HP

MW00910242

by
R. Ray Depew

Grapevine Publications, Inc.
P.O. Box 2449
Corvallis, Oregon   97339-2449 U.S.A.

Acknowledgments

Thanks once again to Hewlett-Packard for their top-quality products and documentation. Thanks also to Chris, Dan and John for their patience, enthusiasm and professional expertise in polishing and presenting this book, a project that stretched across many months and a move to another state.

Pen-and-ink illustrations by Robert L. Bloch.

Printed in the United States of America
ISBN 0-931011-33-7

Second Printing – January, 1992

To my sweet wife, Valerie, in gratitude for her constant encouragement, support and tolerance when things got a little crazy—and for her cookies, which helped me get through the late-night bug-hunts and other tribulations they never tell you about when you start writing a book.

CONTENTS

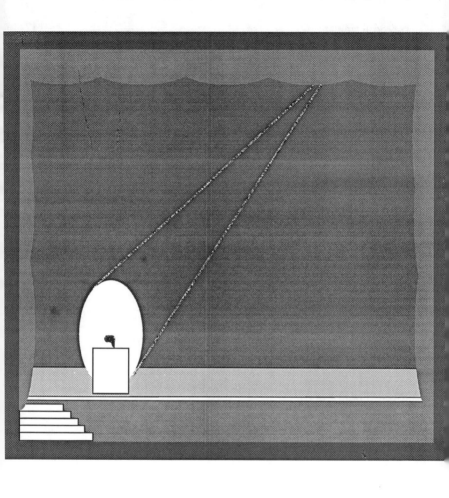

1. INTRODUCTION

What This Book Is About

The HP 48 calculator ("48" for short) is the latest in a long line of great handheld calculators from Hewlett Packard Company. It combines nearly all of HP's most popular features into one package.

The 48 makes handheld problem-solving and/or data manipulation easier than ever before. Among other new capabilities, it offers you the **EquationWriter**, the **Solver**, and the **Plotter**.

- With the EquationWriter, you can enter an equation in *textbook notation*—just the way you normally see it on paper (as opposed to *algebraic notation*, which forced you to count parentheses and put all your terms on one line).

- With the most powerful version of HP Solve to date, you may never have to write another program again: The 48 Solver lets you *solve your equation directly from the equation form,* rather than having to translate it into a program.

- One of the greatest—but most neglected—features of the 48 is its Plotter, and more generally, its graphics capability. You can manipulate the entire 64×131-pixel display, with many powerful built-in functions. And you needn't stop at 64×131 pixels. This book will show you how that display is only a small window into a much larger world of graphics power.

First, take just a moment to see these three capabilities in action. This is just a "warmer-upper" to pique your interest—so don't worry—you'll get more explanation on all of this in the chapters to come....

Plotting a Simple Function

Set your display mode to FIX 2 (2 SPC α α F I X ENTER). Then start with this simple quadratic function:

$$y = (x + 4)(x - 3)$$

To enter the EquationWriter, press ⟵ EQUATION (that's the ⟵ ENTER key). Now, press the following keys (if you make a mistake, backspace it out by pressing the ⬤ "backspace" key, as necessary):

α Y ⟵ = ⟵ () α X + 4 ▶ ⟵ () α X − 3 ▶

Your display should now look like this:

```
┌─────────────────────────────┐
│                             │
│                             │
│   Y=(X+4) ·(X-3)▯           │
│                             │
│                             │
├─────────────────────────────┤
│PARTS│PROB│ HYP │MATR│VECTR│BASE│
└─────────────────────────────┘
```

Press ENTER to exit the EquationWriter and put your equation onto the Stack. Start the PLOT application by pressing ⟵ PLOT.... The first page of PLOT menu keys will appear on the bottom line of the display.

Now store your quadratic equation by pressing the **STEQ** menu key. The Status Area at the top of the display should say:

```
Plot type: FUNCTION
EQ: 'Y=(X+4)*(X-3)'
```

To enter the Plotter itself, press **PLOTR** now. Then press (NXT) **RESET** ←(PREV), to reset the plotting parameters to their defaults.

Next, enter the *x*-domain (the desired range of *x*-values). Use a domain of, say, –5 to 5: Press 5 (+/–) (SPC) 5 **XRNG**

Now you can simply let the 48 calculate the *y*-range automatically and then plot the function—just press **AUTO** ...

The display will blank out, then fill with a parabola as the 48 calculates and plots each point. Now press **LABEL** to label the axes. Your display should then look like this:

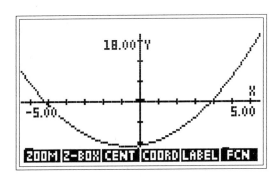

Adjusting Your Plot

Of course, you can change your *y*-range—it doesn't have to be the one that the machine automatically calculated.

Press ATTN. Now, to choose a *y*-range of –20 to 30, type in the coordinates of the lower left and upper right hand corners of the plot: (-5, -20) (5, 30), and press NXT NXT **PDIM** NXT.

Now, instead of pressing **AUTO** , press **ERASE DRAW** ....Your previous parabola is erased, and a new parabola is drawn in its place. Press **LABEL** to label the axes.

But notice this: Press →◄, then press and hold down ▲. The display scrolls down as the cursor travels up the *y*-axis to *y* = 30.... Now where's your parabola? Press and hold ▼ to bring it back into sight. The point here is that you can make your plots *larger than the display*.

So keep in mind that you can use either **AUTO** or **DRAW** to plot the function. **AUTO** will calculate the *y*-range for you—to fit the display. But **DRAW** allows (requires) you to specify your own *y*-range.

Both functions have their uses: For example, use **AUTO** to give you a "feel" for where your function plot will lie. Then use **PDIM** and **DRAW** to stretch or shrink your plotting range, in a way similar to the **ZOOM** functions provided in the PLOT menus (read about **ZOOM** in your 48's Owner's Manual).

Solving Within the Plotter

You can do more with your parabola than just look at it and marvel: Hidden in that display is a graphics cursor, shaped like a crosshair. Press ▼ and ◀ a couple of times to find it.

Now, find out what the two roots of this function are: Press and hold ◀ until the crosshair is close to the left side of the plot, where the function crosses the *x*-axis. Now press **FCN** **ROOT** ....

The crosshair zeroes in on the root and the bottom line of the display tells you that the root is at **-4.00**!

Press ⊟ to get the menu back, and then **SLOPE** to find the slope of the function at this root point (*x* = –4).... The slope is **-7.00**. Now ▼ and ▶▶ to find the cursor, then press and hold ▶ to get to the right side of the screen. Now use **ROOT** and **SLOPE** again to find that the slope at the positive root is **7.00**, as it should be.

Press ⊟ **EXTR** to find the extremum, or lowest point on the function. It's at **(-0.50,-12.25)**. Press ⊟ to bring back the menu, then ◀◀◀ (NXT) **F(X)** to find the function value at the current location.

As you can see, you can utilize most of the capabilities of the Solver *without ever leaving the Plotter application.* And while this quadratic function was admittedly simple, you can do these same things with much more complicated functions—you'll see how in later chapters.

Now press (ATTN)(ATTN) to return to the Stack display.... See? The roots, that you just calculated from inside the Plotter have also been placed on the Stack—for your subsequent use (and calculating enjoyment)!

Freehand Graphics

Using the built-in capabilities of the Plotter and Solver are perfect for many needs. But when you want to create custom graphics of your own, that's a job for the GRAPHICS menu.

Often the 48 gives you more than one way to do things. For example, HP guessed that most people would often use the GRAPHICS menu when a plot was being displayed—so the GRAPHICS menu comes up automatically when you press ▊AUTO▊ or ▊DRAW▊. But you can get to the GRAPHICS menu anytime you want: Press ⌈ATTN⌉⌈◁⌉⌈GRAPH⌉ (do that now).

You've seen the first page of this menu, but press ⌈NXT⌉ and see this:

▊DOT+▊ DOT−▊ LINE ▊TLINE▊ BOX ▊CIRCL▊

Using the ⌈▲⌉, ⌈▼⌉, ⌈▶⌉ and ⌈◀⌉ keys, put the cursor about an inch to the right of the origin. Now press ⌈×⌉ (multiply), then ⌈▶⌉ a few times. You'll see an ✗ where the cursor appeared originally—but now the cursor is sliding to the right. Now press ▊CIRCL▊.... You'll eventually see this:

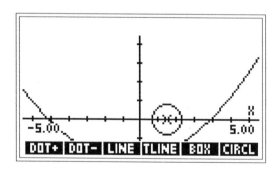

You're doing *freehand drawing* on a plot drawn by the 48!

Next look at the menu items labeled **DOT+** and **DOT−**.

DOT+ turns pixels on (makes them black), while **DOT−** turns pixels off (makes them white). The ☐ annunciator appears in the **DOT+** or **DOT−** menu key label to indicate which one is active.

Experiment with **DOT+** and **DOT−** by pressing each once...then twice...while moving the cursor around....

See? If **DOT+** is activated, to deactivate it, press the **DOT+** menu key once more. The annunciator will turn off—so you can move the cursor about freely, without trailing a black line behind you. In the same way, if **DOT−** is activated, press **DOT−** a second time to move around without erasing whatever images you've just finished making.

Grobbing Around

For the next exercise, press (ATTN) until you return to the Stack. Now, carefully type (without quotation marks):

GROB 3 6 103070304040 (ENTER)

You should see Graphic 3 x 6 on Level 1 of the Stack. Now press the following keys:

(PRG) DSPL PICT (STO) (←) (GRAPH)

You should see a small arrow in the upper left corner of the display, like this:

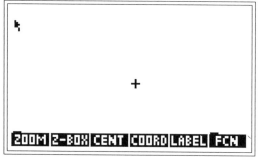

You've done freehand drawing without even using the GRAPHICS menu. (Actually, you have created a *grob*—more on that soon.)

Is It Real—Or Is It...?

Now, just for fun, press [ATTN] to return to the Stack display. Then fill the lowest four levels of the Stack with any objects you want, and press the following keys:

[PRG] **DSPL** [NXT][NXT][NXT] **LCD→** [NXT] **PICT** [STO][←][GRAPH]

Look at the menu. That's the first page of the GRAPHICS menu.... What's it doing in the Stack display?

Press [NXT] once. If the **DOT+** annunciator isn't on, press **DOT+** once to turn it on. Then use the arrow keys to move the cursor around the display.... You're drawing all over your Stack display!

The secret? You're not really drawing on the Stack display (and you can confirm this by pressing [ATTN] to return to the real Stack display). Rather, you've created a *grob image* of the Stack display—and stored it in the graphics display. The advantages of this feature for documenting your programs and creating friendly output should be obvious—and you'll see other uses for this later on, too!

What Next?

By this time, hopefully, you've gotten a taste—and whetted your appetite—for what the 48 can do. Of course, it would take *several* books to tell you all the great things it can do, but this book is to show you how to use the new graphical features in the 48.

To do that, this book is divided into three parts:

1. Beyond-the-Manual Basics

To give credit where credit is due, HP has carefully documented just about every feature they built into the machine. But face it—it's hard to *show* you everything a new application can do in a manual of any reasonable size. So that's what the first part of the book will do with the graphical features:

Chapter 2 should help you be more comfortable—and more effective—with the **EquationWriter**.

Chapter 3 shows you how to unlock the *real* power of the **Solver**. You have already seen how it looks in its "Sunday best"—running inside the Plotter—but wait until you see it "getting down and dirty," in its work clothes!

Chapter 4 teaches you the basics—the "care and feeding"—of **grobs**, the *graphics objects* in the 48. You'll learn how to conjure them up and manipulate them as easily as any other object.

2. Advanced Use—the Graphics "Power Tools:"

Chapters 5-7 go beyond the basics. To help you in effectively using graphics, you'll build a toolkit of convenient and useful routines for storing and recalling grobs, combining text and graphics, etc.

Next, you'll see how to use those tools: You'll tip your head sideways and learn how to do "sideways plotting"—strip charts, waveforms and the like. And you'll see how to create and use freehand graphics in the display.

3. Full-Blown Applications:

Chapters 8 and **9** present several self-contained applications that use programmable Plotter and Solver commands.

Some of these applications are useful as is, while others are offered in hopes that you'll then alter them for your own purposes ("Oh wow—if I change that one subroutine I can ...").

Keep in mind, however, that this book is not necessarily meant to be read from cover to cover. Here are a few suggestions....

Notes on Using this Book

Of course, read this book with your 48 by your side. You needn't do every example or program here, but it's a lot easier to try things—or clarify them—right away, rather than waiting until later, when you've forgotten what was so mystifying and/or exciting.

Also, if this is your own personal copy of this book, then by all means, write in the margins, inside the covers, etc. Make the book useful to *you*. Keep a highlighter and a notepad handy—and use them.

First Note: As you can tell from those opening "warmer-upper" keystrokes, *this book assumes that you already know a few things* about your 48. You should know how to:

- **Name** objects, **edit** them, **store/recall** them—and how to **manipulate** them on the Stack (e.g. SWAP or DROP them, etc.);

- Use **menus** and **menu keys**—and the NXT and ◁ PREV keys;

- Use the MODES menu to set display and calculations modes;

- Use **directories** and "move" through a **directory structure**;

- Build **strings**, **algebraic expressions/equations**, **binary integers**, and **programs**.

This book may occasionally offer reminders on some of these basics, but that's about it. For a good tutorial on all these sorts of topics, read

An Easy Course in Using the HP 48

This book is available from your HP dealer or from the publisher.

Or, if you simply need some "brushing-up" as you go, here's how to use your 48 Owner's Manual ("OM") alongside this book:

- First, carefully reread the OM's chapter called "Objects" (that's Chapter 4)

- Even if your first impression of the EquationWriter ("EW") wasn't exactly thrilling, at least work through the examples in Chapter 16 of the OM. The EW is something new—far ahead of other machines—and its only shortcoming is its speed (for best results, keep a stack of homemade oatmeal-chocolate-chip cookies nearby, to pass the time while the 48 redraws the display).

- Before you start on Chapter 3 here, skim once more through chapter 17 in the OM (just work through the examples they provide). The basic Solver is easy to learn, and once you understand it, Chapter 3 in this book will be much more useful.

- When you've reached the end of Chapter 3 here, you're ready for a serious intermission. Watch some mental junk food on network TV. Eat some real junk food. Eat some real food. Take a nap.

- When you come back, reread Chapters 18 and 19 in the OM. Then work through Chapter 4 here, to learn the fundamentals of grobs—and some "good habits" you should consider adopting.

- After that, you can pick and choose among the remaining chapters in this book. If you don't understand something, come back to Chapters 2-4—or to the index of the OM—for help. If something here is still unclear, write to the publisher.

Second Note: There are 4 kinds of "features" in any computer—including the 48:

- **Documented Features**. Designed features described or at least mentioned in the Owner's Manual.

- **Undocumented features**. Designed features which work predictably—and sometimes usefully—but nevertheless don't make it into the Owner's Manual for various reasons.

- **Unsupported Features**. Features or operations that HP "accidentally" left accessible to users but were never intended for use by the general buying public. These features can greatly enhance your calculator's capabilities, but their misuses often carry drastic consequences (e.g. `Memory Clear`). So these features are neither encouraged nor documented by HP.

- **Bugs**. A bug is simply a design mistake in program code. A bug's behavior may be predictable or erratic, but its consequences are undesirable. If you find a bug in your 48's operation, report it at once to HP. If you find a bug in any code in this book, please write to the publisher.

This book will use primarily **Documented Features**, so that all its examples and programs will work on all 48's. You'll also encounter a small handful of **Undocumented Features** that HP publicized after the manuals were written—plus a couple of **Bugs**.

Third Note: The procedures, examples and programs in this book won't hurt your 48. None of the ideas and procedures described should give you the dreaded Memory Clear (if you get such a message, retrace your steps very carefully, to see where *you* went wrong). In general, if you fear memory loss—for whatever reason—it's a good idea to back up your valuable files frequently.

All the examples in this book worked on 48 ROM version A. If you use them exactly as they appear in this book (forgiving typos), they should work fine on your 48 as well. But feel free to experiment, too. Try some things differently from the way the book does it, and see if you can improve on the ways you see them done here.

Fourth Note: Go!

2. THE EQUATIONWRITER

Preparations

First, you need to create a directory for this chapter—so you don't clobber anything you may already have going:

Press →(HOME), then type 'G.CH2' ←(MEMORY) **CRDIR** (VAR) **G.CH2** to get into this brand-new **G.CH2** directory.

The menu items should now all be blank, and the Status Area at the top of the display should show **{ HOME G.CH2 }**

Opening Remarks

The EquationWriter (EW) is one of the 48's most exciting features—perhaps setting it apart from all other handheld machines. In a world that turns on legal questions of "look and feel," the EW display may *look* like some brand-x displays you've seen, but it *feels* quite different.

Its one drawback—and you might as well recognize it right now—is this: The EquationWriter is SLOW. This may be enough to deter you from using it (a matter of personal choice) but at least read this chapter before deciding. Often the slowness doesn't matter.

Ever since the first FORTRAN compiler or BASIC interpreter let you enter equations on a digital computer, you've been forced to cram the normal, two-dimensional equations you're used to seeing on paper (i.e. *textbook notation*) into the single line of display characters (*algebraic notation*) understood by the software. There had to be a better way....

There *is* a better way: Even with the EW's not-so-blinding speed, it will usually take you far less time to enter an equation correctly into the EquationWriter than with the "algebraic" form.

As you discover this, you'll probably go through these three typical stages with the EW:

- **Excitement & Delight:** "Wow—look at what this can do!" Typically, this lasts about twice as long as it takes you to work through the EW chapter in the Owner's Manual.*

- **Frustration & Discouragement:** Fed up with its slowness— or not yet completely understanding it—many are tempted to abandon the EW in favor of the Command Line editor. These people may have as much trouble trying to debug their algebraics but they don't realize it, having accepted line editors and their attendant frustrations as the cost of machine algebraics.

- For those who survive, there's the third stage, characterized by your high school band teacher's pet motto: "Proficiency comes through practice" (translation: **"Use It Or Lose It"**).

Actually, the EW and the Command Line Editor (CLE) are *both* useful in certain situations: If the EW's slowness bothers you, then use it strictly as an equation <u>writer</u>, or <u>viewer</u>, but not as an <u>editor</u>.

---

*By the way, have you worked through that chapter yet? If not, put a bookmark—not a cookie— here, and go do all the examples in that chapter.

So What Does It Do?

When you write an equation on paper...

$$\int_{b^3-4.32}^{a^3+1} \frac{\sqrt{\dfrac{x^3 - 22x + 1}{\ln x + x}}}{3\ln x + e^{x-4.2}} \, dx$$

...you use this *textbook notation,* an easy way for your brain to understand the problem: It detects *visual patterns* (position, size, enclosure, etc.) to give you an immediate grasp of what's being said.

Compare that with the computerized *algebraic notation* for the above expression:

```
∫(b^3-4.32, a^3+1, ∫((x^3-22*x+1)
/(LN(x)+x))/(3*LN(x)+EXP(x-4.2)), x)
```

It's not so clear at one glance, is it? So the EW lets you enter and view the expression in whichever notation you prefer (inside the 48 it's always represented the same way, no matter which way you enter it).

Then, after you've entered the equation, the EW also provides several tools for manipulating and modifying it. It can even recognize *parts* of the equation to modify, using the properties of algebra and calculus!

Examples

Like the Command Line, you can use the EW to write *algebraic expressions*, *equations* and *unit objects*. An algebraic expression is half an equation; an equation is two algebraic expressions joined by an equal sign (=). For example, the positive root of a quadratic equation is this algebraic expression:

$$\frac{-B + \sqrt{B^2 - 4AC}}{2A}$$

How would you enter this, using the EW?

To Do This	**Press This**
Enter the EW and start a numerator.	⬅ EQUATION ▲
Use Ⓨˣ instead of Ⓧ²—it looks better.	⊟ α Ⓑ ⊞ √x̄ α Ⓑ Ⓨˣ ②
Close the exponent.	▶
Forgetting to close subexpressions with ▶ is a common EW error!	
Imply a ⊗ between a number and the letter following it. The letter is taken as the start of a variable or function name.	⊟ ④ α Ⓐ ⊗ α Ⓒ
Close the subexpression opened by √x̄.	▶
Close the numerator/start the denominator.	▶
Again, imply the ⊗.	② α Ⓐ
Close the denominator.	▶
Place the expression onto the Stack.	ENTER

Complex *unit* objects are also easy to assemble with the EW. Look, for example, at:

The universal gas constant, R:

$$R = 8.315 \frac{\text{J}}{\text{mol} \cdot \text{K}}$$

The gravitational constant, G_c:

$$G_C = 9.8 \frac{\text{kg} \cdot \text{m}}{\text{s}^2 \cdot \text{N}}$$

To enter R using the EW:

[←][EQUATION][8][.][3][1][5][→][_]
[←][UNITS][NXT][ENRG][J][/]
[←][UNITS][MASS][←][PREV][MOL][×]
[←][UNITS][NXT][TEMP][K][▷]

(_ denotes a unit object)

Then press [ENTER] to put this constant onto the Stack.

To enter G_c:

[←][EQUATION][9][.][8][→][_]
[←][UNITS][MASS][KG][×][←][UNITS][LENG][M][/]
[←][UNITS][TIME][S][yˣ][2][▷][×]
[←][UNITS][NXT][FORCE][N][▷]

Then press [ENTER] to put this constant onto the Stack.

Using the EquationWriter

This would be a good place to insert a table of all the keystrokes used in the EW. But your HP Owner's Manual already has a complete table—and the Quick Reference Card has a keyboard diagram. Anyway, to be really proficient with the EW, just remember these…

Rules of Thumb:

- ▶, ▲ and ◀ (not ◀) are the most frequently used keys in the EW.

- Use ▲ to start a numerator, then ▶ to finish it and start the denominator (incidentally, ▼ acts identically to ▶).

- ▶ finishes all subexpressions ("it slices…it dices"):

    It finishes powers, as in y^x

    It finishes numerators and starts denominators

    It finishes denominators and exit the fraction

    It finishes square roots and other roots: $\sqrt[x]{y}$

    It finishes mathematical functions, such as sin (x)

    It jumps to the next parameter when constructing a derivative, an integral or a sum

    It exits a parenthesized subexpression, such as $a + (b + c)$

    It finishes *any* pending subexpression (and →▶ finishes <u>all</u> pending subexpressions).

- ⬅ is the only real editing key you have. Each time you press ⬅, it "undoes" the last keystroke in the equation. Press it repeatedly to go as far back in the equation as you want (the pause is always longest after the first press).

- If you notice an error deep inside your equation, your options are limited. *Do not* press ◀ in an attempt to move the cursor to the error and correct it (◀ takes you to the *Selection Environment*— an upcoming topic).

- Most analytical functions, such as those in the MaTH menu and the powerful IFTE function, work inside the EW. If a function requires parameters, you enter the function, then the parameters, separated by [SPC], and finally ▶ to close the parameter list. For example, to enter the function IFTE(A, B, C), you would press [PRG] **BRCH** [NXT] [NXT] **IFTE** (α)(A)[SPC](α)(B)[SPC](α)(C)▶.

- All the UNITS menus work inside the EW.

There are 3 ways to exit the EW:

- [ENTER] puts the equation on the Stack as an algebraic, then exits gracefully.

- ⬅[EDIT] gives up in disgust and slams the (usually) unfinished equation into the Command Line for further editing. After editing, you can press [ENTER] to return to the EW, and [ENTER] again to place the equation onto the Stack.

- [ATTN] is the "panic button." It dumps the whole thing into the waste basket and escapes to the safety of the Stack display.

The Selection Environment

If you accidentally pressed the ◄ key while practicing with the EW, you may have noticed that you had to wait a terribly long time for the display to do anything. Go ahead—try it now—then go get a cookie....

When the smoke finally clears, you'll find that you can now use the arrow keys to drive very quickly around the equation, highlighting various terms and operators along the way. You'll also see this menu:

RULES| EDIT | EXPR | SUB | REPL | EXIT

This is the Selection Environment, where you can easily select various parts of the equation you're building, to edit or rearrange them.

The last menu item, **EXIT**, simply sends you back to the normal EW display—but look at what the other menu items do for you:

RULES is a compilation of rules for algebraic manipulation—to let you massage the form of your equation or expression.

EDIT and **EXPR** generally work together to let you select the high-lighted portion of the equation and throw it onto the Command Line for individual editing. You can then press (ENTER) to put this edited expression back into your equation, or (ATTN) to abort the edit and return to the EW.

Try one—key in the Ideal Gas Law:

$$pV = nT\left(8.315\frac{J}{mol \cdot K}\right)$$

Now press ◀ and use the arrow keys to move the highlight around, pressing **EXPR** occasionally. Notice these things:

  If the first · is highlighted, **EXPR** includes P · V.

  If the = is highlighted, then **EXPR** includes the whole equation.

  If the _ is highlighted, **EXPR** includes the unit object.

  If the ——————— is highlighted, then **EXPR** includes just the units.

  If the · between mol and K is highlighted, **EXPR** includes only the denominator of the units.

  Pressing **EXPR** a second time highlights only the operator (but pressing **EXPR** when a term is highlighted doesn't do anything).

SUB extracts a copy of the highlighted operator, term or expression and puts it on the Stack. **REPL** replaces the highlighted term or expression (but not operator) with the object on Stack Level 1.* These are useful when you have an often-repeated sub-expression, or when you want to modify only a small part of the equation.

---

*WARNING: **REPL** copies, then drops the object on Level 1. It's gone. ⟵ LAST STACK can get it back for you, but it will also undo your last equation-editing session.

A Fourier Series Example

Here's a fun equation for playing with the PLOT functions, so key it in now as EW practice. This is the Fourier Series representation for a full-wave rectified sine wave:

$$f(t) = \frac{2A}{\pi} - \frac{4A}{\pi} \sum_{n=1}^{N_{max}} \frac{\cos n\omega t}{4n^2 - 1}$$

where A is the amplitude of the wave, ω is its frequency, and N_{max} is the highest harmonic you want to include (see MULTIPLOT in Chapter 8 for an application which uses N_{max}).

You should be able to enter that equation into the EW without much trouble, but here are a few reminders to help:

- Enter f(t) as just plain f (α⟨⟩F).

- π is ⟨⟩SPC.

- Use ⱳ (α⟶W)—not ⱳ—for ω (omega).

- Enter the summation as ⟶TAN α⟨⟩N ▶ 1 ▶ α α N ⟨⟩M ⟨⟩A ⟨⟩X α ▶ COS α⟨⟩N × α⟶W × α⟨⟩T ▶ ÷ 4 × α⟨⟩N y^x 2 ▶ ⟨⟩ 1

- Don't use 4 x² for the $4n^2$ term. Instead, use 4 α⟨⟩N y^x 2 ▶.

Work at this until you get it. Then press ENTER to put the completed equation onto the Stack, and name it FOYAY: ' α α F O Y A Y α STO.

Test Your Skill

At this point, you should have worked through the EW examples in the Owner's Manual. If not, do it—now. Then here's a simple self-test:

The classical expression for the behavior of a series RLC circuit is

$$v = L\frac{dI}{dt} + IR + \frac{1}{C}\int_0^t I\, dt$$

1. Enter this equation with the EW and store it as RLC.

2. Rewrite the equation as

$$v = L\frac{d}{dt}\left(I_0 e^{st}\right) + I_0 e^{st} R + \frac{1}{C}\int_0^t I_0 e^{st}\, dt$$

and save it as RLCEXP (for RLC EXPonential).

3. Rewrite the equation as

$$v = L\frac{d}{dt}\left(A_0 \sin \omega t\right) + A_0 \sin \omega t R + \frac{1}{C}\int_0^t A_0 \sin \omega t\, dt$$

and save it as RLCPER (for RLC PERodic).*

Turn the page to see the EW solutions....

*There. That takes care of about 25% of your undergraduate electronics textbook. The 48 can now solve symbolically for any one of the variables, via ISOL. It can simplify the equations by solving the integral and the first derivative, and differentiate or integrate, too. But that's for another book.

Solutions

1. Press ⬅EQUATION to enter the EquationWriter, then:

α⬅V⬅=αL➡∂α⬅T▶α I▶+α I×αR
+1÷αC▶➡∫0▶α⬅T▶α I▶α⬅TENTER

You should then see   `'v=L*∂t(I)+I*R+1/C*∫(0,t,I,t)'`
at Stack Level 1.

Press `'`αα RL Cα STO to store this.

2. ⬅EQUATION enters the EW. Then press α I α⬅O⬅eˣα⬅S
⊙ ×α⬅TENTER, to put the expression   `'Io*EXP(s*t)'`
onto Stack Level 1.

Now press ENTER ENTER VAR **RLC** ▼, then ◀ to the first I, and
press **REPL**. Next, ▶ to the second I, and press **REPL**; then ▶
to the last I, and press **REPL** ENTER.

On Level 1, you should now see

`'v=L*∂t(Io*EXP(s*t))+Io*EXP(s*t)*R+1/C*∫(0,t,`
`Io*EXP(s*t),t)'`

(The line breaks will be different than those shown here.)

Press `'`αα RL C EXPα STO to store this.

3. $\boxed{\leftarrow}$ $\boxed{\text{EQUATION}}$ enters the EW (alternatively, you could do the entire problem at the Command Line—always keep this in mind).

Then press $\boxed{\alpha}\boxed{\text{A}}\boxed{\alpha}\boxed{\leftarrow}\boxed{\text{O}}\boxed{\text{SIN}}\boxed{\alpha}\boxed{\rightarrow}\boxed{\text{W}}\boxed{\times}\boxed{\alpha}\boxed{\leftarrow}\boxed{\text{T}}\boxed{\text{ENTER}}$, to put

$$\text{'Ao*SIN(}\omega\text{*t)'}$$

onto Stack Level 1.

Now press $\boxed{\text{ENTER}}\boxed{\text{ENTER}}\boxed{\text{VAR}}$ **RLC** $\boxed{\blacktriangledown}$, then $\boxed{\blacktriangleleft}$ to the first I, and press **REPL**. Next, $\boxed{\blacktriangleright}$ to the second I, and press **REPL**; then $\boxed{\blacktriangleright}$ to the last I, and press **REPL** $\boxed{\text{ENTER}}$.

On Level 1, you should now see

$\text{'}\upsilon\text{=L*}\eth\text{t(Ao*SIN(}\omega\text{*t))}$
$\text{+Ao*SIN(}\omega\text{*t)*R+1/C*}\int\text{(0,t,Ao*SIN(}\omega\text{*t),t)'}$

(The line breaks will be different than those shown here.)

Press $\boxed{\text{'}}\boxed{\alpha}\boxed{\alpha}\boxed{\text{R}}\boxed{\text{L}}\boxed{\text{C}}\boxed{\text{P}}\boxed{\text{E}}\boxed{\text{R}}\boxed{\alpha}\boxed{\text{STO}}$ to store this.

How did you do on this little self-test?

If you need more practice, do it now, on your own—or go back over the examples in the HP Owner's Manual, or read Grapevine's <u>Easy Course in Using the HP 48</u>.

Other Things

Here are a few other EW tidbits to know:

Printing: If you press ⟨ON⟩ and ⟨PRINT⟩ simultaneously, you can print out the current EW equation.

However, ⟨STO⟩⟨ENTER⟩⟨SWAP⟩⟨←⟩⟨PRINT⟩ **PR1** will give you a better print-out, especially for long equations (the HP 82240B printer even provides cutting lines for splicing together composite printouts).

Viewing: If your equation is larger than the 131×64 display, pressing ⟨←⟩⟨GRAPH⟩ from inside the EW will let you *scroll* your equation across the display, using the arrow and right-shifted arrow keys. Then just press ⟨ATTN⟩ from scrolling mode to return to the normal EW display.

Closing Remarks

One of the best uses for the EW is to build—and later, to view—your own libraries of equations, constants and units. That way, you won't have to decipher the algebraic notation used on the 48 Command Line and in the rest of the world. A single glance in the EW will tell you everything you need to know about the equation.

Hopefully a faster version of the EW is in the offing, but until then, don't give up on it too easily. Remember the words of Mr. Whetstone, your high school band teacher: "Proficiency comes through practice."

3: THE SOLVER

Opening Remarks

This is the most sophisticated Solver HP has yet produced. The more you use it, the more valuable you'll find it to be. In many cases, the problems you used to solve by writing programs can be handled more easily and quickly with the Solver.

The Solver is indeed like another programming language. In the past, you had to translate the equation(s) into a program, which consisted of a list of data and operations to perform on the data. But compared to this Solver, those ingenious and sophisticated programs you used to use now appear clumsy, slow—and incredibly complicated.

Of course, to do such equations, you can still write step-by-step programs for the 48, but after reading this chapter, you may decide to save your programming skills for more worthy challenges.

Preparations

First, you need to create a directory for this chapter—so you don't clobber anything you may already have going:

Press ⮕(HOME), then type 'G.CH3' and ⬅(MEMORY) **CRDIR** (VAR) **G.CH3** to get into this brand-new **G.CH3** directory.

The menu items should now all be blank, and the Status Area at the top of the display should show this: **{ HOME G.CH3 }**

Apples and Oranges

Suppose you go to the store to buy some fruit. Apples cost $.29 each; oranges cost $.89 each—and you have $20.00 to spend. How many of each can you buy?

Obviously there are many possible combinations, and the Solver is ideal for this, because it lets you play "What-If" in your mind: *"If I buy 3 apples, then I can get that many oranges; if I buy 10 apples, then I can get this many oranges..."*, etc.

So here's the equation to type and (ENTER) onto the Stack:

TOTAL=CSTA∗APPLES+CSTO∗ORANGES

Then store this equation under the name 'Fruit', and press ←(SOLVE) to enter the SOLVE menu:

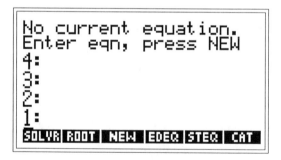

To tell the 48 to use the Fruit equation as the *current equation*, just type the name, 'Fruit', and press STEQ. The 48 then stores 'Fruit' into the reserved name, EQ, the *current equation*.

Now you should see this:

```
Current equation:
Fruit: 'TOTAL=CSTA*AP...
4:
3:
2:
1:
SOLVR ROOT  NEW EDEQ STEQ  CAT
```

Press **SOLVR** to get into the Solver itself. Now things are simple:

[2] [0] **TOTA**
[.] [2] [9] **CSTA**
[.] [8] [9] **CSTO**
[→] **TOTA** to recall your $20.00 to Stack Level 1.

Pressing a menu key *stores* a value into a variable name; pressing [→] prior to the menu key *recalls* the value to the Stack; and pressing [←] prior to the menu key *solves* for that variable.

For example, if you buy 8 apples, how many oranges can you buy?
Press [8] **APPL** [←] **ORAN**... ____Result____: ORANGES: 19.87

Or, if you wanted just 5 of each, how much would this cost?
Press [5] **APPL** [5] **ORAN** [←] **TOTA**... ____Result____: TOTAL: 5.90

Of course, you could add other items to the equation; the Solver will allow you multiple pages of variable-names; just use [NXT] and [PREV] to page through them all ([→][NXT] is a shortcut back to the first page).

Notice the last item in the SOLVER Menu: **EXPR=**

If your equation is a bona fide, "grammatically correct" equation (two algebraic expressions linked by a =), **EXPR=** will solve for each side of the equation and display the results in Stack Levels 1 and 2. This is useful in cases where an exact solution may be impossible—or unbelievable—and you want to see if the left-hand side really does equal the right-hand side.

If your "equation" is really just an expression, then **EXPR=** will calculate its current value and put this at Stack Level 1.

If you see a special on oranges, say, 6 for $8.00, you can quickly see how "special" the special really is. Just set the number of apples equal to zero and solve the equation for the corresponding cost of one orange:

⓪ **APPL** ⑥ **ORAN** ⑧ **TOTA** ⇦ **CSTO**....

Some bargain—$1.33 each! Better to buy them singly at $.89!

The Ideal Gas Law

For the next example, take something from chemistry and physics—the Ideal Gas law: $P*V=n*R*T$

P is the pressure of the gas

V is the gas volume

n is the number of moles of the gas

R is the ideal gas constant, 8.315 J/mol·K

T is the absolute temperature of the gas.

Enter this equation, using either the Command Line or the EquationWriter, so that you have `'P*V=n*R*T'` on Level 1 of the Stack. Then store it into a variable: `'IdealGas'` [STO].

Next task: Store the value 8.315 into the variable `'R'`, and *include the units*. To do this, you can use either the UNITS menus or the alpha keyboard—and either the EW or the Command Line. Either way, you should get 8.315_J/(mol*K) in Level 1. Then type `'R'` [STO].

Now use the *Equation Catalog* to get your gas equation back. You can get to the Equation Catalog directly by pressing [→][9] (if there were room enough, CAT would be written in blue letters over the [9] key—just to the right of ALGEBRA).

Then use [▲] and [▼] to move the pointer to the IdealGas equation and press **SOLVR**. This is a handy short cut for getting to the Solver or the Plotter—they share the same Equation Catalog!

Now use this equation to calculate the number of moles of air in a typical bicycle tire: For a 27"×1.25" tube, the volume is about 33.13 cubic inches. Use $T = 70°F$, and $P = 80$ psi (but to account for atmospheric pressure, 14.7 psi, you must use 80+14.7, or 94.7 psi).

Press: (9)(4)(·)(7)(←)(UNITS)(NXT) **PRESS** **PSI**
        (→)(LAST MENU) **P** (3)(3)(·)(1)(3)(←)(UNITS) **VOL** **IN^3**
        (→)(LAST MENU) **V** (7)(0)(←)(UNITS)(NXT) **TEMP** **°F**
        (→)(LAST MENU) **T**

Solve for n: (←)**N**.... Result: Bad Guess(es)—an error message.

When working with unit objects, you must store an initial guess for the variable you're solving for.*

So, press (1)(←)(UNITS) **MASS** (←)(PREV) **MOL** (→)(LAST MENU) **N**.
Now try solving for n again: (←)**N**.... Result: n: 1.10_mol

Well, this time you got a result. Too bad it's wrong.

"Say what?"

Yep, it's wrong...

---

*If you get this Bad Guess(es) error while solving for a unit object, press (←)(REVIEW) to get a summary of the contents of each variable and of the current equation. Often, you'll have forgotten to press (←) when *solving* for the unknown, thus inadvertently *storing* some (incorrect) object there instead. **Remember:** Press the unshifted key only to *store* a value in a named variable! (←) *solves* for the variable, (→) *recalls* the variable contents to the Stack.

If you want the Solver to ignore units entirely, then you must (←)(PURGE) all variables named in the equation and re-enter the Solver. That means you're likely to clobber the Gas Constant, R, which is, after all, a variable as far as the machine is concerned. Later in this chapter you'll see how to keep the Gas Constant safe from harm.

This isn't the fault of the Solver, but stems from a quirk in the way **temperature units** are converted. You can read more about this quirk on page 197 of your Owner's Manual. The Solver makes no errors converting other types of units, but it is often suckered into making *relative* instead of *absolute* temperature conversions. And it doesn't tell you it's doing this—it just gives you the wrong answer. To be safe, you should always convert temperatures to Kelvins before using them with the Solver.

So recall the temperature (→ T) and convert it to Kelvins (→ UNITS UBASE) and then recalculate n:

→ LAST MENU   T   ← N   Result: n: 0.14_mol

Now then, for subsequent calculations, if you know that the previous value of the variable has the correct units, then you can just store a numeric value on top of it, and it will assume those same units.

Example: Find out how many cubic inches of air at atmospheric pressure are compressed into that bicycle tire.

OK: Atmospheric pressure is 14.7 psi, so press 1 4 · 7 P to store the value in P—thus using the psi units remaining from last time (you can verify that the units are correct by watching the status line).

Now press ← V to find the volume of uncompressed gas....

          Result: V: 213.43_in^3

The Time Value of Money

Next up—for all you finance wizards—is the Time Value of Money equation.

$$0 = PV + PMT\left[\frac{1-(1+I)^{-N}}{I}\right] + FV(1+I)^{-N}$$

where

PV   is the Present Value of the loan or investment.

PMT is the periodic (monthly, annual, ...) PayMenT.

FV   is the Future Value of the loan or investment.

N   is the Number of periodic payments or compounding periods.

I   is the Interest rate per compounding period.

Build this equation using the EW or the Command Line (the EW is easier) and put it onto Stack Level 1. Then name it—type 'TVoM' [STO].

This TVoM equation is a mainstay of all business calculators, but it comes in handy even for engineers trying to buy houses, figure out their IRA's, or calculate the balances on their student loans.

For example, suppose you want to buy a $65,000 home (no, it's actually quite a nice house—this is Corvallis, Oregon): You have $5,000 for the down payment, and you want to finance the rest at 11.5% for 30 years.

Use the Equation Catalog ([→][9]) to select the TVoM equation (use [▲] and [▼] to move the pointer to it), and press **SOLVR**.

Now, the Present Value is the money you're going to receive right now, $60,000 (OK, you may never really hold it in your hand, but the bank is technically giving it to you to give to the seller). And the Future Value is what you'll owe the bank at the end of the mortgage period—that is, nothing (hopefully). So press $\boxed{6}\boxed{0}\boxed{0}\boxed{0}\boxed{0}$ $\boxed{\text{PV}}$ $\boxed{0}$ $\boxed{\text{FV}}$.

Next, since this is a 30-year loan, with monthly payments, N is 30×12, or 360. And the monthly interest rate will be 11.5%÷12, or 0.115÷12. So press $\boxed{3}\boxed{6}\boxed{0}$ $\boxed{\text{N}}$ $\boxed{\cdot}\boxed{0}\boxed{0}\boxed{9}\boxed{5}\boxed{8}\boxed{3}\boxed{3}$ $\boxed{\text{I}}$ to enter the number of payments and monthly interest.

Now just press $\boxed{\Leftarrow}\boxed{\text{PMT}}$ to find that your monthly payment is $594.17. The minus sign means that it's money subtracted from your pocket.

Notice that both the Ideal Gas and the Time Value of Money equations use variables named N or n. So after you've used each equation, you'll see not one but two $\boxed{\text{N}}$ labels in your VAR menu. You can press $\boxed{\Leftarrow}\boxed{\text{REVIEW}}$ from either the $\boxed{\text{VAR}}$ menu or from the Solver variable menu to see which is which (or—if it really bothers you—store the two equations in separate sub-directories inside the G.CH3 directory).

Anyway, since you've used a capital N for one and a small n for the other, the Solver can tell them apart, and that's the main thing. But if you use the identical variable N in two separate equations in the same directory, *beware*—especially if either uses a unit object: You'll get all sorts of nasty messages until you purge the unit-object N.

A Third-Degree Polynomial

The general form of a third-degree polynomial is

$$a*x^3+b*x^2+c*x+d$$

Key in this expression and store it as `'POLY'`.

To find its roots, you set it equal to zero and solve for x. Of course you can easily do this within the Plotter, as you saw in Chapter 1. But if you only want one root—or a specific root lying between two known values—the Solver alone is often faster.

Take the polynomial $x^3+ 2x^2-5x-6$. You know by inspection that it has at least one positive and one negative root (right?... right?...).

Press **CAT** (remember? →9), move the selection arrow to POLY and press **SOLVR**. Now, enter the coefficients: 1 A 2 B 5 +/− C 6 +/− D.

Solve for a root by pressing ← X.... You should get x: −3.00.

If that's the only root you need, you can stop there. To solve for the positive root, give some huge positive number as a first guess for x, then solve for x: 1 0 0 X ← X....   Result: x: 2.00

And of course, as long as you've gotten this far, why not solve for the third root?

The Solver lets you enter up to *three guesses* for an unknown quantity:

- If you enter one guess, such as ⓪ ▣ X ▣, then ⇦ ▣ X ▣ takes that guess as the starting point and moves from that point towards the actual root.

- If you enter two guesses, such as ② ⋅ ⑨ +/- ▣ X ▣ ① ⋅ ⑨ ▣ X ▣, then ⇦ ▣ X ▣ calculates the function at both guesses and judges by those results whether to stay within the bounds of the guesses or to go outside them.

- If you enter three guesses, such as ① +/- ▣ X ▣ ⋅ ⑨ +/- ▣ X ▣ ① ⋅ ② +/- ▣ X ▣, then ⇦ ▣ X ▣ uses the first value as the "best guess" and the other two values as the probable bounds of the search.

As you might imagine, it's often difficult to find the third root unless your initial guesses are very close, and that's where the Plotter becomes extremely useful: In the Plotter, all you have to do is get the crosshairs close to the root in question and press **FCN** **ROOT** from the Plotter menu!

Customizing the Solver

Keeping the Gas Constant a Constant

Looking back at your **IdealGas** equation, you just *know* that sooner or later, someone will accidentally press ▢**R** (instead of →▢**R**) when checking the value of the Gas Constant. So it would be better if you could take it off the Solver menu altogether—preventing access to it there. And you can do this: You can design your own variable menu for use with your equations, omitting variables that don't vary—like the Gas Constant. To do so, just put your equation into a list, like this:

```
{ 'p*V=n*R*T' { p V T n } }
```

In this list, the equation comes first, followed by a list of the variables that you *do* want to appear. Notice that you can put these variables in any order—maybe with the most frequently used variables first (this saves a lot of time if you're solving an equation with more than one menu page of variables).

Put the above list on Stack Level 1, and press ←SOLVE **NEW**. You'll then be asked to name the equation and press ENTER. Since your "equation" is now a list object, *you must append* **.EQ** to the name so the Solver will recognize it. Happily, the 48 provides the **.EQ** for you here; all you have to do is type **IdealGas** ENTER, as before.... The Status Area should show

```
Current equation: IdealGas.EQ: { 'p*V=n...
```

Press **SOLVR** to see your customized menu that hides ▢**R**:

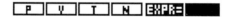

Running Programs from Inside the Solver

The variable Solver menu list structure can also include *executable programs*. In the Ideal Gas law, for example, suppose you're using your 48 to monitor the amount of gas in a pressurized reactor. The volume and temperature are constant, and you can calculate the quantity of gas from the measured pressure. Hypothetically you'd have a functional program, READP, to read a pressure sensor and put the value onto the Stack. But to simulate that process here, just use a trivial READP (Checksum: # 45658d   Bytes: 37.5)—a constant: « 5_atm »

So replace P in your variable list with a list of this form: { "*menu label*" { « *prg1* » « *prg2* » « *prg3* » } }. The "*menu label*" is the label that will appear on the menu; « *prg1* » is the program that its *unshifted* selection will execute. « *prg2* » and « *prg3* » are the programs that the ⬅- and ➡-shifted selections of this item will execute, respectively (but these are optional; you can ignore the shift keys and simplify your list to { "*menu label*" « *prg1* » }).

Let the unshifted menu key be the call to READP. Therefore « *prg1* » will be « READP DUP 'P' STO 1 DISP 1 FREEZE ». This reads the pressure, stores it into the variable name 'P', and displays it in the Status Area—just as the Solver would do for a value that you keyed in. Then « *prg2* » will be an empty ("do-nothing") program, « », since you don't plan to *calculate* the pressure. And « *prg3* » will be « P », to recall the value in P to Stack Level 1—just as any other ➡-ed variable key would do in the Solver.

Thus, the list to replace P becomes { "P" { « READP DUP 'P' STO 1 DISP 1 FREEZE » « » « P » } }.

Now clear the Stack ($\rightarrow$CLR) and then type VAR $\rightarrow$ **IDEAL** ▼ to edit a copy of IdealGas.EQ. When you've finished, your list should look like this:

```
{ 'p*V=n*R*T' { { "p" { « READP DUP 'p' STO 1 DISP
  1 FREEZE » « » « p » } } V T n } }
```

Press ENTER to put it onto the Stack. Store it as 'REACTOR.EQ'. Then start the Solver and select REACTOR.EQ as the current equation. The Solver display looks a little different, as shown here:

If you REVIEW the variables, you'll see only V, T and n, since p is no longer a Solver variable (notice that the ▮▮**P**▮ item is white-on-blue, instead of the blue-on-white). This is how the 48 helps you differentiate between variables and programs in the menu. Try the unshifted and shifted ▮▮**P**▮ key to see how it works....

The unshifted key displays '5_atm' in the status line (and notice that with a slightly more elaborate program in the variable list, you could make it display p: 5_atm).

The $\leftarrow$ key does nothing (as you intended), and the $\rightarrow$ key puts the value of 'p' onto the Stack.

A More Versatile TVoM Equation

The next thing to change is your TVoM equation a little bit (look back on page 48 to see the original). As always when customizing with the Solver, the idea is to make it easier to use:

- First, include a factor to account for when the payments are made (i.e. the beginning or end of the month). This factor is a multiplier to the PMT:

$$0 = PV + (1 + I * Begin?)PMT\left[\frac{1 - (1 + I)^{-N}}{I}\right] + FV(1 + I)^{-N}$$

  Begin? will be a true/false variable, with a value of 1 if payments are made at the beginning of the month, or 0 (the default) if payments are made at the end of the month.

- Next, change all occurrences of I to I/100. This way, you can enter 5% interest as ⑤ ⬛, instead of ·⓪⑤ ⬛.

- Finally, to accommodate interest compounded quarterly or monthly, introduce a variable called Per (periods per year)—the number of compounding periods in a year (12 for monthly payments, 4 for quarterly, 1 for annual, etc.).

  Thus, since N is the number of years, N*Per will be the total number of periods—and payments. And I/(100*Per) will be the interest per compounding period.

By now, the TVoM equation is a monster. In textbook notation, it is:

$$0 = PV + \left(1 + \frac{I*Begin?}{100Per}\right)PMT\left[\frac{1-\left(1+\dfrac{I}{100Per}\right)^{-NPer}}{\dfrac{I}{100Per}}\right] + FV\left(1 + \frac{I}{100Per}\right)^{-NPer}$$

Or, in algebraic notation, it is:

```
0=PV+(1+I*Begin?/(100*Per))*PMT*((1-(1+I/(100*Per))^
-(N*Per))/(I/(100*Per)))+FV*(1+I/(100*Per))^-(N*Per)
```

Yep, that's right: *You* get to build this, using whichever method you wish—EW or Command Line—to edit the current version of TVoM (quiz: which method would *you* rather use?).   Go...

Finished? OK, now if you were to store this equation (don't do it yet), the Solver would give you seven variables to juggle, plus the **EXPR=** item besides. But you can make the equation a bit more friendly, by attaching this variable list to it:

```
{ N I PV PMT FV { "SETUP" { « VIEWP » « MQA »
« BEGEND » } } Per Begin? }
```

No—you don't need to re-enter the equation. Using your list-building process, just put the current monster TVoM equation on Stack Level 2, the variable list on Level 1, then press ② PRG **OBJ** **→LIST** ....and save the whole thing in 'TVoM.EQ'.

You now have a full-fledged Solver "program". Select it from the equation catalog (either ← SOLVE **CAT** or → ⑨) and start the Solver.

You should get a display like the one below.

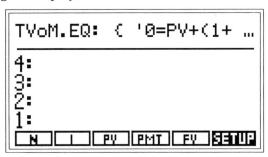

```
TVoM.EQ:  {  '0=PV+(1+  ...
4:
3:
2:
1:
   N  │    │ PV │PMT │ FV │SETUP
```

This version of TVoM is more "friendly" than the first one: On the first page of its two-page menu are the commonly-used variables, plus a **SETUP** menu key. **SETUP** serves three functions.

Unshifted **SETUP** will run a program called VIEWP (for "view parameters"), which displays the current settings of the variables Per and Begin?: If Per has a value of 1, 4 or 12, the first status line will show ANNUAL, QUARTERLY or MONTHLY, respectively; if Per has any other value, say 5, the first status line will show 5 PERIODS/YEAR. And, if Begin? contains zero, the second status line will show PMTS AT END; otherwise it will show PMTS AT BEGINNING.

← **SETUP** will run a program called MQA to rotate the Solver through monthly, quarterly or annual payments. And → **SETUP** will run the program BEGEND, which toggles the value of Begin? between 1 and 0. Both MQA and BEGEND call VIEWP to update the display.

The second page of the variables menu gives you direct access to Per and Begin?, so you can set bimonthly payments or calculate interest compounded daily—when Per must have a value other than 1, 4 or 12.

Here are the three programs, VIEWP, MQA and BEGEND:

```
                VIEWP
Checksum:  # 14516d
Bytes:     415.5

« IFERR 'Per' RCL
  THEN DROP MQA 'Per' RCL
  END
    → per
    « IF 'per==4'
      THEN "QUARTERLY"
      ELSE
          IF 'per==12'
          THEN "MONTHLY"
          ELSE
              IF 'per==1'
              THEN "ANNUAL"
              ELSE
                  Per IP →STR
                  " PERIODS/YEAR"
                  +
              END
          END
      END
    »
    1 DISP
    IFERR 'Begin?' RCL
    THEN DROP BEGEND
        'Begin?' RCL
    END
    → begin
    « IF 'begin'
      THEN "PMTS AT BEGINNING"
      ELSE "PMTS AT END"
      END
      2 DISP 1 FREEZE
    »
»
```

```
                MQA
Checksum:  # 17323d
Bytes:     164

« IFERR 'Per' RCL
  THEN DROP 1
  END
    → per
    « IF 'per==1'
      THEN 4
      ELSE
          IF 'per==4'
          THEN 12
          ELSE 1
          END
      END
    »
    'Per' STO VIEWP
»
```

```
              BEGEND
Checksum:  # 34006d
Bytes:     90.5

« IFERR
      'Begin?' RCL
  THEN DROP 0
  ELSE NOT
  END
  'Begin?' STO VIEWP
»
```

Linking Equations: Solving Several at Once

For this next topic, go back to your "Apples and Oranges" equation. Suppose you've borrowed your nephew's little red wagon—which can hold only 50 pounds—to haul your groceries home. How many apples and oranges can you afford—and still be able to get them home?

Hmm…to avoid exceeding either your budget or your wagon's capacity, you now have two problems. The first is already taken care of by your existing Fruit equation:

$$TOTAL=CSTA*APPLES+CSTO*ORANGES$$

But now there's this new equation (key it in and store it as 'Wagon'):

$$LOAD=WT.A*APPLES+WT.O*ORANGES$$

The Solver lets you *link* equations in order to solve several at once. To use this feature, you combine the equation names in a list and give the list a name ending with .EQ (just as you did when modifying the TVoM equation—this .EQ ending is used for all non-algebraic objects to be used with the Solver).

So create the list { Fruit Wagon }. To do this, you can either type it in directly or press ⤶ { } VAR ⤶ PREV **FRUIT** NXT **WAGO**. Then ENTER it and store it as 'Load.EQ'.

(Note that the Equation Catalog also comes in handy like this, when you're creating lists to link more than two simple equations.)

Now select `'Load.EQ'` and start the Solver. Your display will look like the one below.

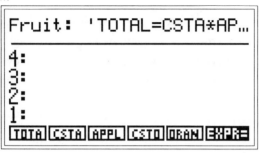

```
Fruit:  'TOTAL=CSTA*AP...
4:
3:
2:
1:
TOTA CSTA APPL CSTO ORAN EXPR=
```

Notice that the Solver is ready to work on the first equation in the list, `'Fruit'`. But press NXT and notice the new menu label: **NXEQ**. Press **NXEQ** now to see what it does.

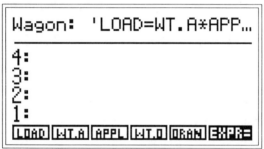

```
Wagon:  'LOAD=WT.A*APP...
4:
3:
2:
1:
LOAD WT.A APPL WT.O ORAN EXPR=
```

Get the idea? If you have several equations in your list, such as { EQ1 EQ2 EQ3 EQ4 }, **NXEQ** bumps EQ1 to the last place in line, moves all the other equations up one place, { EQ2 EQ3 EQ4 EQ1 }, and sets up the Solver to work on EQ2.

Now press **NXEQ** a few times until the Solver returns to `'Fruit'`. It's time to test all this!...

Press $\boxed{\leftarrow}$$\boxed{\text{REVIEW}}$ to see that each variable in 'Fruit' has an assigned value (the values in the examples at the beginning of this chapter should still be there: CSTA should contain 0.29, and CSTO should contain 0.89).

Now press $\boxed{\text{NXEQ}}$ to go to the 'Wagon' equation. Apples are about three to a pound, so press $\boxed{\cdot}$$\boxed{3}$$\boxed{5}$ $\boxed{\text{WT.A}}$ to enter an apple's weight. Now imagine some big, juicy oranges—about a pint each: Enter $\boxed{\cdot}$$\boxed{5}$ $\boxed{\text{WT.O}}$. Solve for the total weight by pressing $\boxed{\leftarrow}$$\boxed{\text{LOAD}}$....

For another variation on the problem (and to further demonstrate the "What-If?" nature of the Solver), how much would it cost to fill your wagon with an equal weight of apples and oranges?

Press $\boxed{2}$$\boxed{5}$ $\boxed{\text{LOAD}}$ $\boxed{0}$ $\boxed{\text{ORAN}}$ $\boxed{\leftarrow}$$\boxed{\text{APPL}}$....   Result: Apples: 71.

Then press $\boxed{0}$ $\boxed{\text{APPL}}$ $\boxed{\leftarrow}$$\boxed{\text{ORAN}}$....   Result: Oranges: 50.

Then $\boxed{5}$$\boxed{0}$ $\boxed{\text{APPL}}$ $\boxed{7}$$\boxed{1}$ $\boxed{\text{ORAN}}$, then $\boxed{\text{NXEQ}}$ to get back to the costing equation, and $\boxed{\leftarrow}$$\boxed{\text{TOTA}}$....   Result: TOTAL: 77.69

That's the cost of a wagonful of equal weights of apples and oranges.

Another good example of a set of linked equations is this set for linear motion:

$$v = v_0 + at$$

$$x = x_0 + \frac{1}{2}(v_0 + v)t$$

$$x = x_0 + vt + \frac{1}{2}at$$

$$v^2 = v_0^2 + 2a(x - x_0)$$

Enter these four equations and store them into 'M1', 'M2', 'M3', and 'M4', respectively.

Then store the list { M1 M2 M3 M4 } into 'MOTION.EQ'.

Now you can solve for x, x_0, v, v_0, a and t, if you know any three of them: You store the three (or more) known values and then use ▉▉▉▉ and ⟵ REVIEW to cycle through the equations, solving each one in turn, until there are no more undefined variables.

Solving with linked equations does have some limitations:

- The Solver won't search for undefined variables nor define or solve for them automatically. For example, if you define everything but the variable ORANGES in the Fruit equation—so that its value is implied—then solve for LOAD in the Wagon equation, you'll still get the error message: Undefined Variable(s).

- In some iterative methods using more than one equation, the order of solving the equations determines whether the solutions converge or diverge. The Solver cannot help you avoid diverging solutions.

Fortunately, there are two workarounds for these limitations:

- Since the Solver is programmable, you can automate much of the process for use in analysis and design of iterative solutions.

- Second, the Multiple Equation Solver application in the HP Solve Equation Library Card can solve for all the unknowns in a system of equations, given the necessary minimum number of independent variables.

For most of your needs, the normal interactive Solver is sufficient, but if you need more, stay tuned for more information on programmability—or invest in an HP Solve Equation Library Card!

Using the Solver on Ill-Mannered Functions

Earlier versions of the Solver accepted only "well-mannered" functions; you couldn't use Solver with square waves, step functions, or other real-world functions. For those, you had to resort to programming.

Well, no more. The 48's Solver can handle it all. The key to making it work is to *think ahead*. Plan out exactly how you'll approach your problem from the start. With planning and practice, you can now make the Solver do what used to require a lot more programming.

Try it: For the step function $y = \begin{Bmatrix} 1 \text{ where } x \geq x_0 \\ 0 \text{ where } x < x_0 \end{Bmatrix}$, write a simple

program:
```
« IF 'X≥X0'
    THEN 1
    ELSE 0
    END
»
```

Next, name the program, say, 'Step.EQ'
(Checksum: # 29349d   Bytes: 54).

Then select it for use with the Solver, and see:

Just as with an algebraic equation, the Solver examines the program, extracts variable names and builds a variable menu from those names. And as you've seen, you can "lock in" values by specifying a variable list and omitting the fixed values. For example, change `Step.EQ` now to

```
{ « IF 'X≥X0' THEN 1 ELSE 0 END » { X } }
```

Now x_0 is omitted from the menu, so that the Solver appears as

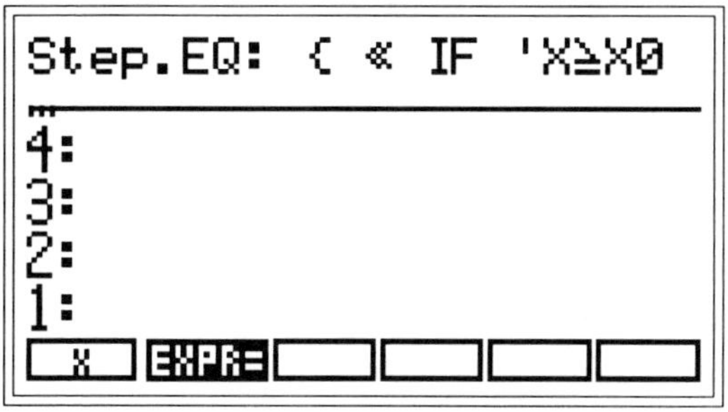

Of course, this function is ill-mannered; it can't be differentiated: Trying to do so onto the Stack with [→][∂] gives a `Bad Argument Type` error; trying it in the Plotter via FCN F' gives `Invalid EQ`.

Even rewriting the program as a user-defined function doesn't help:

```
« → x x0 « IF 'x<x0' THEN 0 ELSE 1 END » »
```

This still isn't written as an algebraic, and the 48 can differentiate only algebraics. But also in the [PRG]-BRCH menu—on the very last page—is IFTE, which *can* be used in algebraics. For example, the above step function can be rewritten simply as `IFTE(X<X0, 0, 1)`—that's all there is to it. And IFTE can be differentiated and integrated—like a constant coefficient that passes transparently through the differentiation or integration.

One problem that has vexed engineers for years—and led to many ingenious programs—is how to model a real diode. A diode is a kind of electronic "One Way" sign, ideally allowing infinite current flow in one direction (called *forward bias*) and zero current flow in the other direction (called *reverse bias*). Here's a plot of voltage vs. current for an ideal diode:

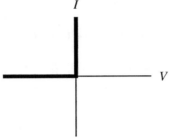

Well, a real, solid-state diode isn't quite that good:

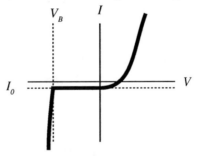

Typically, the transition from forward to reverse bias takes place at *about V* = 0 volts. Under reverse bias ($V < 0$) the current is fairly constant at I_0 = 1 picoampere to 1 microampere. Under forward bias ($V > 0$), the diode current follows this relation:*

$$I = I_0 \left(e^{\frac{V}{.0259 \text{ volts}}} - 1 \right)$$

*This assumes a constant temperature of 300 K. A good electronics text will give you temperature-dependent expressions for both I and I_0.

If the reverse bias voltage exceeds a given value V_B, or *breakdown voltage*, then the diode loses all effectiveness and becomes essentially a short circuit—current is very high.

So a good diode equation should model all three areas of the *V-I* curve, and it should be continuous. It can be done using two nested IF...THEN...ELSE commands in a program—or two nested IFTE functions in a single equation:

$$I=IFTE(V<Vb, 1E99*V, IFTE(V>0, Io*(EXP(V/.0259)-1), -Io))$$

Type this in and call it DIODE (<u>Checksum</u>: # 44495d <u>Bytes:</u> 127). This matches the diode model very well and maintains a continuous function through the three regions of forward bias, reverse bias and breakdown.

For example, a typical diode has these characteristics:

$$I_0 \quad = \quad 10^{-6} \, A$$
$$V_B \quad = \quad -10 \, V$$

Storing these two values completely defines your diode—and since the variables are naturally arranged in the variable menu, you don't even need to create a variables list!

The Care and Feeding of derFN

It may seem strange to have a section on functions in the middle of the Solver chapter, but such considerations of ill-behaved functions are important for using the Solver inside the Plotter—coming up next.

In many cases you will find it easier to differentiate an equation and solve for the variables in the resulting first-derivative equation. But if your original equation contains several functions for which the 48 cannot find a derivative, it will indicate this by creating a dummy derivative and listing the variables available to solve the problem.

Press `'`(MTH)**PARTS** **ABS** (α)(X)(ENTER), then `'`(α)(X)(ENTER)(→)(∂). You'll get the algebraic function `'SIGN(X)'`. Now press `'`(α)(X)(ENTER)(→)(∂) again, to get the function `'derSIGN(-3, 1)'`.

> _"Where did this come from?"_ you may well ask.

To answer your question, repeat the calculation, but this time create the algebraic `'∂X(SIGN(X))'` and press (EVAL). This time you get: `'derSIGN(X, ∂X(X))'`. Now you can see what happened in the first case: instead of stopping at a symbolic representation of the differential, the 48 went on and completely evaluated the variables, replacing X with -3 (currently stored in X) and calculating the derivative of a constant (1). Press (EVAL) again to see this substitution.

Moral: If you want to completely evaluate a derivative in one step, use the Stack method. For symbolic representation of the derivative or for _stepwise differentiation_, include the derivative into your algebraic and evaluate to the level you need. See your HP OM (pages 420-422) for more details.

Now, next question: What is this derSIGN all about?

This is the 48's way of saying "I don't know how to differentiate the function SIGN(X), but I'll use these placeholders for X and dX until you show me how the derivative should be defined."

You'll probably face the same problem with many of your own user-defined functions. When you use **FCN** **F'** on one of these functions, if the 48 can't find a numerical approximation to the derivative, it will give you a nasty message and give up.

You can avoid this by trying all your derivatives beforehand. If you find a derFN somewhere in your differentiated expression, then you should consider how the function should be differentiated.

For example, with SIGN(X), it's obvious that 'derSIGN(X, dX(X))' is zero everywhere but at $x = 0$, where it is infinitely large. So you could create the function « → x dx 'IFTE('x==0', 1E499, 0)' » and store this as 'derSIGN'. When you evaluate derSIGN after defining it, you'll get a result of 0 (assuming -3 is still stored in X).

SIGN is a *unary* function—it acts on only one argument; percent is an example of a *binary* function—it acts on two arguments:

The derivative of '%(X, Y)' with respect to Z is:
$$\text{'der\%(X, Y, }\partial Z(X), \partial Z(Y))\text{'}$$

Pages 422-423 in the Owner's Manual gives a solution for 'der%'. Work out other *user-defined derivatives* in the same manner.

Using the Solver Inside the Plotter

The 48 Solver really shines inside the Plotter application, where it's even more versatile than in its stand-alone form.

For this example, start with your POLY equation (be sure that a, b, c and d still contain 1, 2, -5 and -6, respectively). Enter the Equation Catalog either by pressing [←][PLOT] **CAT** or via the [→][9] shortcut. Scroll down the list until the pointer is beside POLY, and press **PLOTR**.

Once inside the plotter, PURGE the name 'x'. Then press [NXT] **RESET** to reset all plot parameters to their default values. Press [←][PREV] ['][α][←][X] **INDEP**, then **AUTO** to see what happens....

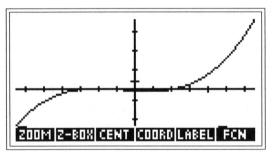

No big deal, right? And you use the **ZOOM** commands to get to the interesting part of the curve:

The menu in the display is the GRAPHICS menu (you saw this briefly in Chapter 1). Press [◄][◄] to find the graphics cursor. Then press and hold [◄] until the cursor is above and to the left of the leftmost root. Press **Z-BOX** to mark the point. Now press and hold [►] to move the cursor past the rightmost root, then press and hold [▼] until the cursor is about four pixels below the x-axis.

Now press **Z-BOX** a second time. The Plotter will redraw the function:

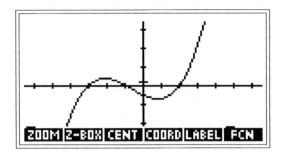

Reminder: Press [ATTN][◄][ATTN][◄] to toggle between the Stack display and the current plot. Pressing [◄] sends you from an idle Stack display (i.e. no Command Line or interactive Stack) to the graphics display. Pressing [ATTN] returns you to the Stack display. Also, pressing [←][◄] will go to the graphics display from *almost anywhere*; the [◄] shortcut is worth remembering.

Press **FCN** to see the Solver and other *function analysis tools*. The Solver is built into the first two of these menu items: **ROOT** and **ISECT**.

With **ROOT** (as described in Chapter 1), you use the [▲][▼][◄] and [▶] keys to position the graphics cursor near where the curve crosses the *x*-axis, then press **ROOT**.

Try finding the three roots of POLY: –3, –1 and 2....

There are some significant differences between the way that the Solver application works in its stand-alone form and the way it works within the **ROOT** operation:

- The stand-alone Solver solves for any variable you want, but the **ROOT** version solves for the value of the independent variable which makes the dependent variable go to zero. To solve for a different variable using **ROOT**, you must change independent variables from the PLOTR menu. For example, to specify the variable a as the independent variable, you must type ['] [α] [←] [A] (or [VAR] ['] **a**), then **INDEP**.

- Another difference is that the Solver will display *intermediate results* for you if you press any button except [ATTN] while it's thinking ([ENTER] is probably the easiest key to find while you're watching the display). The Solver tells you, with a short message, how it arrived at the answer, and it puts the numeric result onto the Stack with the variable name for a tag.

  ROOT, by contrast, doesn't give you intermediate results or a message, but it does position the cursor exactly on the intersection (useful for subsequent operations like **SLOPE**). Also it puts the result onto the Stack as a real number—with the tag Root: —and displays the numeric result on the graphics display until the next keystroke.

- If the function does not have a real root, such as with $'Y=X^2+2'$, the Solver finds a local *extremum* (minimum or maximum). It then puts that *x*-value onto the Stack and the Extremum value in the Status line.

  ROOT puts the closest approximation onto the Stack and flashes **EXTREMUM** on the graphics display, positioning the cursor at the extremum of the function and displaying the numeric result.

- Note that in some cases (as in the $'Y=X^2+2'$ example cited here), the Solver and **ROOT** will return slightly different values of X for the extremum.

- **ROOT** can return results that are difficult or impossible to coax out of the Solver. If the Solver's answers don't make sense, enter the Plotter, declare your unknown as the independent variable, and solve for it graphically. And note that if EQ contains a *list* of two or more equations, then the Plotter will plot all the functions, but **ROOT** will find the roots of the *first* equation, and **ISECT** will find the points of intersection between the *first two* equations in the list.

The majority of equations you'll plot have an isolated variable on the left of the equals sign—or no equals sign at all. But you may occasionally have an equation such as this:

$$15 - 2x^2 = x^2 + 3x + 5$$

The Plotter treats this equation as two separate algebraics, separated by an equals sign; it plots them both.

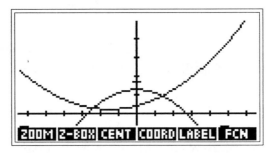

ROOT finds only the point where the right hand side of the equation equals zero. In order to find the roots of the equation, you must use **ISECT** to find the point(s) where the two function plots intersect.

Of course, you can get around this by subtracting the left side from the right side to get an equation of the form $' \mathbf{0} = \mathbf{fn}(\mathbf{X}) '$, but sometimes you do want to see both sides of the equation separately.

Look at some other items on the FCN menu. At first glance, you might think that **SLOPE** and **F'** do the same thing, but not quite: **SLOPE** computes the slope of the function *at the cursor location* (though the cursor need not be right on the curve; it will "home in" on the curve once the result is computed and displayed).

F' computes *and plots* the derivative of the equation *at every x-value* in the plot range. It also adds the equation for the first derivative to the list in EQ (or, if EQ only contains a single equation, then **F'** creates a list with the new equation inserted at the start of the list). To see this, use your POLY plot (pages 70-71)—the **Z-BOX**'ed version:

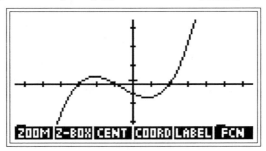

Now, pressing **FCN** [NXT] **F'** adds a parabola to the display, since the first derivative of a cubic function is a quadratic:

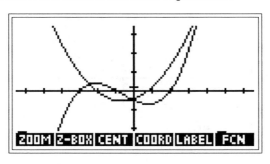

And EQ is now this list: { '3*x^2+2*(2*X)-5' POLY }

Press ■ **F'** two more times (give each press time to draw)....

The list in EQ becomes

$$\{ \ 6.00 \ \ '3*(2*X)+4' \ \ '3*X^2+2*(2*X)-5' \ \ POLY \ \}$$

And the next two derivatives—a slanted line and a horizontal line—appear on the display:

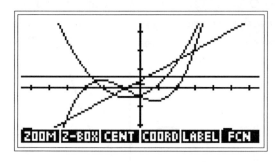

The item labelled as **NXEQ** simply makes the next equation in the EQ list the current ("first") equation. For example, after you have pressed **NXEQ** twice, your display should look like this:

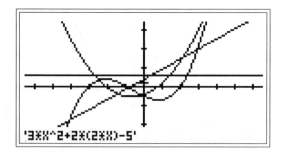

The "first equation" is now the parabola.

For unruly equations, such as $15 - 2x^2 = x^2 + 3x + 5$, **NXEQ** will swap the left-side and right-side expressions, and all **FCN** operations will then act upon the new right-hand side.

Keep in mind that you can switch back and forth between the Plotter and Solver at any time—and use **NXEQ** in either application. And keep in mind also that if you alter any other variables used in the equations, you must redraw the graphics display (by pressing **ERASE DRAW** in the Plotter menu).

FCN simply returns the function value at the current cursor location. For unruly equations, **FCN** returns the value of the right-hand side; the Plotter's **FCN** is the graphical analog of the Solver's **EXPR=**.

EXTR returns the coordinates of an extremum of a curve—but it won't tell you if it's a maximum or minimum. With POLY, pressing **EXTR** with the cursor just to the left of the origin returns this display:

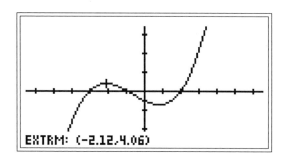

EXTRM: (-2.12,4.06)

AREA performs a numeric integration on the "first equation" in EQ, with respect to the *x*-axis. To perform the integration, you just position the cursor near the starting point, and press **AREA** or ⊠ to mark one limit. Then position the cursor near the other limit and press **AREA**.... It takes awhile, and you get only the labeled integral, but it's easy to do.

Try It: Find the area under the curve between the greatest and least roots of POLY.

Move the cursor near the smallest root and press **ROOT** ⊟ **AREA**. Then move the cursor near the greatest root and press **ROOT** ⊟ **AREA**. You'll see:

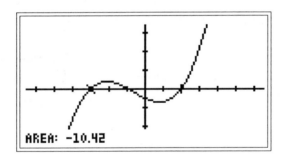

AREA: -10.42

Programmable Use of the Solver

There will be occasions when you need to use the Solver *in the middle of a program* (as opposed to the other way around). The commands STEQ and RCEQ are indeed programmable. If you want a user to be able to store or solve for variables *interactively* during the program, you can include the following commands in your program.

To store the equation into EQ and invoke the Solver:

$$\ll \text{ ... } \text{ 'eqname' STEQ 30 MENU HALT ... } \gg$$

When the 48 encounters this, it will store the variable name `'eqname'` into EQ, activate the SOLVR menu (menu number 30) *and halt program execution* (the status line will display **HALT**). You can then use the Solver to store values or run other programs from inside the Solver variable menu—then press ←[CONT] when you're ready to continue the program.

Alternatively, to *avoid halting* the program during the Solver, simply use the ROOT command. Of course, to do so, you need to set up the Stack so that ROOT finds the arguments it needs:

Stack inputs:
- **3:**   Symbolic or Program object (the equation)
- **2:**   Global variable name
- **1:**   Real, Complex, List or Unit object (the first guess)

Stack outputs:
- **1:**   Real, Complex or Unit object (the answer)

Here's an example of using ROOT. This is a program that calculates monthly payments for a 5-year, $15,000 loan at different interest rates. The program (AMRT: <u>Checksum</u>: # 28425d   <u>Bytes</u>: 226) uses the original TVoM equation (page 48) and invokes ROOT to print a table of payments and interest rates:

```
« 15000 'PV' STO 0
  'FV' STO 60 'N' STO
  .05 .15
  FOR int int DUP
     12 / 'I' STO 3
     FIX →STR "→ " +
     'TVoM' 'PMT' -100
     ROOT 2 FIX →STR +
     PR1 DROP .01
  STEP
»
```

A more polished version would provide prettier output, but at least this program illustrates the power of ROOT in a program. You could also use ROOT to calculate loan amortization schedules. Try it (and then compare it to AMORT in the HP Solve Equation Library, if you have it— you may not be able to beat its speed, but probably its versatility).

Another example idea: You can easily combine

```
« ...'IdealGas' STEQ 30 MENU HALT...
»
```

                          and

```
« ...xxx.xx_mol 'n' STO
  'IdealGas' 'p' 1_atm ROOT...
»
```

to solve for partial pressures of gases in a plasma chamber or tower.

Review

Okay, set down your calculator, grab a handful of cookies, and think for a moment about the 48 Solver application.

You heard it suggested at the start of this chapter that it's really another programming language—even another programming environment. And you've seen the acrobatics the Solver can do:

- You learned how to customize the Solver menus to fit your needs, how to protect variables and perform "outside" tasks from inside the Solver.

- You saw how the Solver is integrated with the Plotter application, and you learned about differences between the graphical Solver and the stand-alone Solver.

- You were introduced to using the Solver within a program.

As you can see, if your work relies on mathematics to any degree, the 48 Solver can greatly reduce the amount of « ...programming... » you do. The HP Solve Equation Library contains 300 prewritten equations covering dozens of different topics—and new equation libraries are being compiled constantly.

Of course, « ...programming... » isn't dead; there will always be needs for it. But now the Solver can do many of the things that formerly *had* to be done in a « program ». So get comfortable with the Solver—using a handheld calculator/computer has never been so easy!

4: WHAT'S A GROB?

Opening Remarks

With its ability to manipulate complex information in the forms of objects, the 48 makes it easy for anyone to do serious graphics on a handheld machine—something not possible before. Other handhelds have "large" screens or dot-matrix displays but nothing as accessible or versatile as the 48 *grob* (its proper name is "**gr**aphics **ob**ject," but the 48 shortens this to *grob*).

A Clean Slate

Before you start, set up your machine for some good, hard graphics work:

- First, in your **HOME** directory, create a directory called **TOOLS**, to store your programs.

- Then, in that **TOOLS** directory, create another directory called **PICS**, where you'll store your grobs and do your graphics work.

This will prevent you from clobbering other object names and prevent both your **HOME** directory and working directory (**PICS**) from becoming too cluttered. So from now on (unless specifically directed otherwise), store all programs in **TOOLS** and all grobs in **PICS**. And when actually *using* (executing/evaluating) any program or grob, do so from **PICS**.

Now it's time to talk about grobs....

What *Is* a Grob?

A grob is simply another way for the 48 to store data. You're already familiar with matrix objects, program objects, character string objects, complex number objects, etc.

A grob is just another kind of object—a pixel-by-pixel description of an image that can be displayed on the 48 display, or passed to another 48 or PC, or "dumped" to a printer. A grob can also be manipulated or combined with other grobs—just as other objects can be manipulated and combined in various ways.

Create a simple grob to experiment with—plot a sine wave:

If you're not in RADians mode, press ⊖RAD. Then press ⏽ SIN α X
ENTER ⊖PLOT **NEW** ENTER **PLOTR** NXT **RESET** ⊖PREV **AUTO**.

The graphics display should fill with a sine wave—big deal.

Press ATTN to exit graphics mode.

Move into your new **PICS** directory, and then press PRG **DSPL** **PICT** →RCL 'SINE' STO.

PICT is the reserved name in which the 48 stores the current graphics display (much as EQ is the reserved name in which the 48 stores the current equation). Therefore, PICT can be STO'ed and RCL'ed, but it cannot be deleted (yes, you can PURGE it, but a new PICT will be automatically created if you then plot a function or press ←GRAPH). So make a mental note: Don't use PICT as an object name, because the 48 has reserved that name for its own use.

In the above exercise, **PICT** →RCL placed the grob representing the current graphics display onto Stack Level 1. Then 'SINE' STO stored it under that name in your **PICS** directory.

Now take a closer look at this grob. Press VAR **SINE** ▼, and you'll see GROB 131 64, followed by a mass of characters.

What do all those characters mean? To get a better idea, compare them with an "empty" grob: Press ENTER →PLOT **ERASE** to clear the graphics display, and then PRG **DSPL** **PICT** →RCL 'EMPTY' STO to store the blank display as an object called 'EMPTY'. Now VAR **EMPTY** ▼ (or VAR **'EMPTY** VISIT) to see GROB 131 64, followed by a mass of zeros.

This is the Stack's representation of a grob. The word GROB simply tells you that the object is a grob. The second "word", 131, is the number of *columns* of pixels (dots) in the grob. The third "word", 64, is the number of *rows* of pixels in the grob. And then the huge "word" after that is a hexadecimal bitmap of all the pixels themselves, where every digit represents 4 pixels.

Pixel Numbers vs. User Units

A grob's size is normally expressed as "*m* pixels wide by *n* pixels high." For example, the display grob PICT has a normal default size of 131 pixels wide by 64 pixels high. But you can also express such dimensions in *user units*. User units allow you to define the scale and limits of PICT in more convenient units—to save you a conversion between Cartesian coordinates and pixel locations every time you want to modify PICT.

To illustrate this, return the SINE grob to the graphics display and view it, by pressing (VAR)(') SINE (→)(RCL)(PRG) DSPL PICT (STO)(◄).

Each pixel in this 131×64 grob is defined by a list of two binary integers, of the form { # col # row }. These are "pixel coordinates." Here are a few pixel locations expressed in their pixel coordinates:

```
┌─────────────────────────────────────────────────┐
│ ─{ # 0d # 0d }                                   │
│                           { # 125d # 10d }─      │
│                                                  │
│      { # 65d # 27d }──                           │
│                                                  │
│                                                  │
│                              { # 130d # 63d }╲   │
└─────────────────────────────────────────────────┘
```

However, recall that when you plotted the sine wave, the 48 used the default *x*-axis range of –6.5 to 6.5, and it assigned the *y*-axis range to be –1.3 to 1.0. These ranges were in user units.

A graphical location in user units is expressed in the form of a complex number, (x, y). Here are the same four locations as on the previous page, but expressed in user units rather than in pixel coordinates:

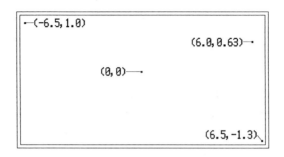

Comparing the two diagrams, notice that their scales behave differently: The pixel coordinate scale always starts at `{ # 0d # 0d }` in the upper left-hand corner, and the numbers increase as you proceed downward and to the right. But the user-units scale starts at whatever values you (or, by default, the 48) have defined, and these numbers increase as you move *up*ward and to the right.

So, which scale should you use? Obviously, user units are much more convenient in many respects. You do your computations, you plug in the numbers, you plot them—just as on graph paper.

Anyhow, HP has made the plotting commands versatile enough to accommodate both scales. And the (PRG) **DSPL** functions **PX⇒C** and **C⇒PX** allow you to quickly convert from one scale to the other if you want to see both sets of the numbers.

But performing grob manipulations with user units does have a couple of disadvantages. First of all, it's slower. The 48 doesn't "think" in user units. When you give it a graphics command with real or complex arguments, it has to find out what the current graphics scale is, then convert the arguments to binary integers (pixel coordinate values) and then execute the command. This can increase your program execution time by as much as 50 percent.

Secondly, user units don't always remain the same. They can differ from directory to directory and program to program, as you redefine them. So always check the graphics scale before manipulating grobs, if you're going to do so in user units.

With those considerations in mind, you can see that if your application involves a good deal of plotting and mathematical modeling, then user units are for you. On the other hand, if your application involves placing text in grobs, extensive fiddling with bitmaps, or mixing grobs of unknown user units, then you should stay with pixel coordinates. As a good rule of thumb, if you're doing too many conversions from one scale to the other, it's a sure sign that you need to switch to the other scale.

"Roll Your Own" Grobs

You have several ways to create a grob (i.e. put one onto the Stack):

- **ERASE** (PRG) **DSPL** **PICT** (→)(RCL) creates an empty 131×64 grob.

- To create an empty grob of a *specified size,* use the **BLAN** (BLANK)
  command. You put the number of rows (as a decimal integer) at
  Stack Level 2, and the number of columns (as a decimal integer)
  at Stack Level 1, then press (PRG) **DSPL** (NXT)(NXT) **BLAN**. The
  empty grob will be placed at Level 1.

- To turn any object into a grob, put the object at Level 2 and a real
  number on Level 1. Then press (PRG) **DSPL** **→GRO** (that's →GROB).
  If the real number is 1, 2 or 3, the 48 will use the small, medium
  or large font, respectively, to create the grob. If that argument
  is 0 and the object is an algebraic or unit object, its grob will be
  created in textbook format—as in the EquationWriter.

- (PRG) **DSPL** **LCD→** copies the current display to a grob.

- Both (←)(PLOT) **DRAW** and (←)(PLOT) **AUTO** will create a grob named
  PICT with a function or statistical data plotted on it. To then put
  this grob onto the Stack, you type PICT (→)(RCL) (from the Stack
  display), or (STO) (from within the Graphics display).

- (STO) converts to a grob directly from the EquationWriter.

- You can also create a grob on the Command Line. For example
  (do this now), type GROB 8 2 83FF (ENTER).... See?

The Hexadecimal Bitmap

That grob you just created is 2 rows (of pixels) tall and 8 columns (of pixels) wide. An 8×2 grob therefore has 16 pixels ("picture elements").

A hexadecimal digit*, expressed in binary form, can hold information for 4 pixels. For example, the hex number B (which has a decimal value of eleven), is expressed in binary as 1011. So the hex number B can describe a row of 4 pixels, where all but the second pixel are "on" (dark); the second pixel is "off" (light). Similarly, a hex 0 (binary 0000) would be all pixels "off", and a hex F (binary 1111) would be all pixels "on".

The 48 always uses an *even number* of hex digits for each row. So if your grob is between 1 and 8 pixels wide, you'll need 2 hex digits to describe that row—even if you use only a few of those pixels.

Since each hexadecimal digit represents 4 pixels in a row, it's easy to think of a grob as a collection of 1-row, 4-column bitmaps:

m columns

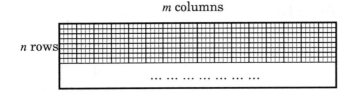

n rows

In the grob you just created (via GROB 8 2 83FF), for example, the digits 83 described the first row of pixels; the digits FF described the second row.

Unfortunately, HP decided that the bitmaps should read backward from the conventional ordering of the digits in a binary number. That is, you might naturally *think* that 83 would describe this bitmap:

hex digit value		8				3		
binary place value	8	4	2	1	8	4	2	1
pixel value	1	0	0	0	0	0	1	1

But no—it doesn't. Rather, the 83 describes this bitmap:

hex digit value		8				3		
binary place value	1	2	4	8	1	2	4	8
pixel value	0	0	0	1	1	1	0	0

Perplexed? It's understandable. This takes some getting used to—and to help that process along, take a look at your grob....

The SEE Program

The 48 doesn't have a quick command to let you "see" the graphics representation of a grob on the Stack, so you need to write one now.*

Notice that **PICT** [STO] takes a grob from Stack Level 1 and puts it into the reserved variable PICT, and that the ⟵[GRAPH] command lets you view and manipulate PICT.** Your Mission: incorporate your observations into a program, 'SEE' (Checksum: # 9380d Bytes: 25).

Solution: « PICT STO GRAPH
           »

> In your TOOLS directory, type this on the Command Line and press [ENTER]. Then type 'SEE' [STO].

> Now, with any grob in Stack Level 1, SEE will let you see it immediately—try it! Use SINE, EMPTY, or your GROB 8 2 83FF—whatever.

Create other grobs using the Command Line, and view them using SEE. Remember: If you use too few digits, the 48 will simply "pad" the grob with zeros, but if you use too *many* digits, it will give you an *error message.*

---

*If you don't know how to write programs on the 48, place a bookmark here, skim over the chapter on "Programming the HP 48" in the Owner's Manual, then return here.

** Yes, you could use the PVIEW command in place of ⟵[GRAPH], but PVIEW requires an argument in Level 1, and it doesn't allow access to the graphics editing menus—not so handy.

What Does a Grob Eat?

A grob eats memory.   Lots of it.

Even a 0×0 grob uses 10 bytes of memory. And how would you make a 0×0 grob to see this?   A couple of different ways, actually:

GROB 0 0 (ENTER)

or

0 # 0 (PRG) **DSPL** (NXT)(NXT) **BLANK**

What's more, if you were to convert that 0×0 grob to a string, `"GROB 0 0"`, it would use *14* bytes.

As you can see, memory use is of primary consideration when you're working with grobs. So here are two quick utilities to help you measure grob size:

GSIZE

<u>Checksum</u>: # 52100d
<u>Bytes</u>:   78

```
«  →  w h
     '10+h*(1+IP((w-1)/8))'
»
```

GSIZE takes the row and column arguments from the Stack and gives you the size of the graphics object itself.

$SIZE

<u>Checksum</u>: # 4548d

<u>Bytes</u>: 130

```
« DUP2 SWAP →STR SIZE
  SWAP →STR SIZE SWAP
  → w h lw lh
  '12+lw+lh+2*h*(1+IP((w-1)/8))'
»
```

$SIZE takes the row and column arguments and gives you the size of the *string* representation of the grob. This is very important to know if you're uploading grobs in ASCII format to another computer; the 48 must have enough memory to hold both the binary and the ASCII representations.

Keep these two utilities in your **TOOLS** directory. They'll help you budget your memory resources as you develop graphics applications. For example, they'll tell you that a screen-sized, 131×64 grob uses 1098 bytes, and its corresponding string uses 2193 bytes. And a 200×200 grob needs 5010 bytes in binary and 10018 in ASCII.

As you can see, grobs eat memory in big bytes.

The Grob as Icon

Grobs that are 21×8 have a special application in the 48. For example, key in the following list of lists (this is all one object, so don't hit (ENTER) until the very end—and ignore the line breaks printed here; there's only so much room on a page):

```
{
{ GROB 21 8
0000000608100904208012404021803C001000000000000 "SINE" }
{ GROB 21 8
000000004801006C81105A4908492504C8130248010000000 "SAW" }
{ GROB 21 8
0000008F1E70801240801240801240801240E0F3C1000000 "SQUARE" }
{ GROB 21 8
0000006775D11555501553D115555506775D1000000000000 "YEAH!" }
} MENU (ENTER).
```

You should see a very interesting menu line. The four grobs you created are acting as the custom menu labels!*

The current term for pictorial display objects like these is "icon." You may be familiar with several icon-based computer interfaces. If you can fit only 4 or 5 characters of text into a menu label, you may one day forget what that label stands for (as in: "Does anybody remember what **EQSP2** does?"). But an icon can often give more information in the same amount of space. A picture is worth a thousand words.

*See Chapter 15 of the Owner's Manual ("Customizing the Calculator") for more information on creating custom menus. You may want to make a note there that 21×8 grobs can act as menu labels.

This example could be the custom menu for a Fourier Series calculation program. You can easily do similarly for electrical circuit elements, insect species, heat exchangers, stars, etc.—the list is endless.

To create an icon, follow these steps:

1. In the graphics environment, press →CLR→◄→▲, then ⊗, then ▼ seven times, then ► twenty times, then NXT ▐BOX▌.

2. Use the freehand drawing keys (see chapters 5 and 7) to draw your icon. Then erase the outline, if you wish.

3. Press →◄→▲, then (if the little × has disappeared) ⊗, then ▼ seven times, then ► twenty times, and then (NXT) ▐SUB▌, to copy your icon to the Stack.

4. Arrange your unshifted (and shifted, if any) key actions on Stack Levels below the icon, specify the Level of the icon, and press PRG ▐OBJ▌ ▐→LIST▌.

5. Repeat as needed to create up to 6 icon lists (or more, to create a multiple-page menu). Finally, give the number of menu items and press ▐→LIST▌ →MEMORY ▐MENU▌.

Review

In this chapter, you created the **TOOLS** and **PICS** subdirectories to hold your grobs and your programs—and to help you organize your thoughts.

You also learned:

- how a grob is represented graphically and numerically—and how much memory it eats;

- how to use the **GROB** *row col nn...* notation, so that you can read or write a grob from the Command Line;

- how to create grobs—both empty or with pre-plotted patterns in them—and how to use them in custom menus.

5: GRAPHICS BASICS

The Graphics Functions

Now that you understand what a grob is and how it is built, return to the built-in graphics functions and run through them briefly. They are all programmable to some degree, and you're going to see that programmability at work now, too.

HP chose to scatter the graphics commands among several different menus (a custom menu might be very handy—food for thought). Some are in the [PLOT] and [GRAPH] menus, some under [PRG]-**DSPL**, and some under [PRG]-**OBJ**. For a reference listing of the graphics commands, see Appendix B.

Now, as you know, you can get to the graphics display by pressing [◄] from the normal Stack display. However, the more general form of the command is [←][GRAPH]—and in a program listing, [←][GRAPH] gives you the GRAPH command, which causes the program to halt in the graphics display with the graphics menu active. Then [ATTN] returns you to the Stack display and continues program execution (note that in a program, the TEXT command also returns you to the Stack display).

To view a grob in the Stack display, put the grob onto Stack Level 1 and use the ⇸LCD command (⎡PRG⎤ **DSPL** ⎡←⎤⎡PREV⎤ **⇸LCD**).

The grob will fill the display with its upper-left pixel in the upper-left corner of the display, overwriting everything except the menu line (and the menu remains active). ⇸LCD does not halt program execution.

To activate the graphics display without the menu line—and still without halting program execution—use the PVIEW command.

PVIEW requires an argument in Stack Level 1—the location of the pixel to be in the upper-left corner of the display. Normally, this would be the row 0, column 0 pixel, so you would put { # 0d # 0d } in Level 1 and press **PVIEW**. Remember that the first number in this list is the column number; the second is the row number. Remember also that, if you wish, you may give the coordinates of the upper-left corner in user units instead, with a complex number (x, y), where you choose the coordinates x and y.

Within the graphics environment, pressing ⎡←⎤⎡GRAPH⎤ a second time removes the menu and puts you in a "scrolling mode." In this scrolling mode, you can use the arrow keys and ⎡→⎤'ed arrow keys to scan around a large grob, with the display acting as a "window" into the grob. In fact, PVIEW is the programmable equivalent of this scanning capability.

Press ⎡←⎤⎡GRAPH⎤ a third time to return to the graphics display, or press ⎡ATTN⎤ to return to the Stack display.

The PVIEW Bug

The PVIEW command is plagued by a bug (in the 48's Rev. A ROM and possibly later revisions). So far, this bug hasn't proven to be seriously harmful, but it's a little disconcerting. To check for it, do this:

1. Type 64 STWS (ENTER), then (→)(#)(1)(ENTER)(+/–).... You'll get:
    # 18446744073709551615d. Store it as TEMP (in PICS).

2. Type GROB 150 150 0 (ENTER) PICT (STO), to put an oversized grob into the graphics display.

3. Create the program « PVIEW .5 WAIT » and put several copies of it onto the Stack (PVIEW is intended for use in a program; this program lets you make sure PVIEW is working properly).

4. Put { # 0d # 0d } onto Stack Level 1 and press (SWAP)(EVAL). You'll see the upper left corner of your grob for just a moment—PVIEW is working properly.

5. Put { # 900d # 900d } onto Level 1 and press (SWAP)(EVAL). You'll see Bad Argument Value, since { # 900d # 900d } is located far outside the defined grob—PVIEW is still working properly.

6. Use TEMP to put { # 18...d # 18...d } on Level 1. This is a location *just one pixel above and to the left* of the grob's upper left corner. Press (SWAP)(EVAL).... Your 48 will freak out for awhile (the results vary), then return to the Stack display, shaken but intact.

PVIEW *should* detect *all* illegal pixel locations—and then display Bad Argument Value to alert you. Well, it does all right when the illegal argument is in user units (a complex number) or in pixel values *much* too large for the grob—but not when the argument is a pixel location *just beyond* the left top edge of the grob.

Workarounds

Since PVIEW works correctly with user units, the simplest fix is to convert all pixel locations to your own user units first. Or, if your programs use PVIEW a lot, use this program (name it PVUE and put it into your **TOOLS** directory; <u>Checksum</u>: # 49037d   <u>Bytes</u>: 36):

```
« IFERR PX→C
    THEN
    END
    PVIEW
  »
```

PVUE converts the argument to user units and traps illegal locations. Unfortunately, it returns the erroneous pixel location to the Stack in user units, and then C→PX won't convert back to the original erroneous pixel values. So here's a version (<u>Checksum</u>: # 17430d <u>Bytes</u>: 88) that *will* return the erroneous pixel location to the Stack (but it won't identify the error as a PVIEW error):

```
« → loc
   « IF loc DUP TYPE 5 SAME
      THEN PX→C
      END
      IFERR PVIEW
      THEN DROP loc ERRN DOERR
      END
    »
  »
```

Anyway, you can at least test the pixel values to see if they're less than # 10000d (that's larger than the size of the largest possible grob, but small enough to get Bad Argument Value instead of the bug). Such a filter reduces your chances of getting caught by the bug.

The Secrets of PPAR

As you read in Chapter 4, every grob has associated with it a height and a width, measured in pixels. The height (rows) and width (columns) appear in the Stack display as   **Graphic** *ccc* ✕ *rrr* or in the Command Line as   **GROB** *ccc* *rrr* *dddd*....

If you ever need to test a grob within a program, the programmable command SIZE returns the number of columns to Level 2 and the number of rows to Level 1.

With that in mind, consider this: Associated with the plotting and graphics routines is a reserved variable named PPAR (for Plot PARameters). Like the reserved variables IOPAR and PRTPAR, PPAR is created (if it doesn't already exist) only when a graphics routine invokes it.

That is, PPAR is invoked or created *anytime you activate the graphics environment, even if you don't see the graphics display.* Specifically, PPAR is invoked by:

- ⟵GRAPH or ◀
- ⟵PLOT or PLOTR
- Any drawing function
- PVIEW with user units (a complex number)—but not with a list of binary integers or an empty list)

And of course, PPAR can be STOed, RCLed and PURGed, like any other variable. The contents of PPAR, however, must follow this pattern:

$$\{ \ (x_{min}, y_{min}) \ (x_{max}, y_{max}) \ \text{indep} \ \text{res} \ \text{axes} \ \text{ptype} \ \text{depend} \ \}$$

You set these 7 parameters from the PLOT menu, or by using the PLOT menu commands inside a program. The default values are:

```
{ (-6.5,-3.1) (6.5,3.2) X 0 (0,0) FUNCTION Y }
```

The short program « PICT SIZE PPAR » will tell you all you need to know about the graphics display—if you can read it. When inside the PLOT application, you can press ⟨⟩ REVIEW to display the plot type, independent variable and grob limits in user units. In a program, the best way to get at the PPAR data is to recall the contents to the Stack and either →LIST or SUB to extract the parts that you need.

Bear in mind that each directory in the 48 has its own PPAR, which can cause you trouble if you work in user units and switch directories a lot.

For example, if you're working in DIR1 where PPAR contains $x_{min}=-10$ and $x_{max}=10$, and then you switch to DIR2 where PPAR contains $x_{min}=0$ and $x_{max}=6.28$, you'll get undesirable results if you use DRAW or any user-unit commands without first adjusting x_{min} and x_{max}.

Generally speaking, you'll need to get only the plotting limits at the start of PPAR. In the next section, you'll see how to get out more information.

The PLOTR Menu

The PLOTR menu consists of 3 pages of commands, listed here:

ERASE	DRAW	AUTO	XRNG	YRNG	INDEP
DEPN	PTYPE	RES	CENT	SCALE	RESET
AXES	DRAX	LABEL	*H	*W	PDIM

Rather than attack the commands by page, group them according to what they do:

You've already met **PTYPE**, **AUTO** and **DRAW**. As mentioned earlier, when DRAW is executed inside a program, it plots a function without adding axes or anything else to the plot.

You are already familiar with **LABEL** as well. Remember that LABEL uses whatever numeric display format is currently active to label the axes (STD format often causes LABEL to include too many significant figures in your plot). LABEL is programmable.

DRAX is a command for drawing axes inside a grob. It is useful inside a program, used in conjunction with DRAW.*

ERASE erases the contents of PICT—and it's programmable.

The more drastic **RESET** resets PPAR to its default values, resizes PICT to its default 131×64 size, and erases the contents of PICT. **RESET** is not programmable, and—unfortunately—it's not recoverable either (i.e. there's no LAST GRAPHICS command). So use **RESET** with care!

---

*For example, the MULTIPLOT program in Chapter 8 uses DRAW and DRAX together, where AUTO obviously wouldn't work.

The other commands in the PLOTR menu give you direct control over PPAR—and they're programmable: **INDEP** **DEPN** **RES** **AXES** **CENT** **SCALE** **XRNG** **YRNG** **PDIM** **✻H** and **✻W**. Also, be aware that →'ed versions of most of these commands will recall the corresponding parameters to the Stack (and although these →'ed functions are not programmable themselves, you can create little programs to do that).

INDEP and **DEPN** (INDEP and DEPND) specify the independent and dependent variables by name. Defaults are X and Y—but those won't work in equations such as `'Impact=(Mass*Speed^2 )/2'`.

You can use a list—instead of just a name—to specify the range over which the function may be plotted. For example, to plot just the first two revolutions (720°) of a spiral, you'd type `{ 'Theta' 0 720 }` **INDEP**. Then you could use small programs to recall those parameters:

« PPAR 3 GET	« PPAR 7 GET
» (independent variable)	» (dependent variable)

RES sets the *resolution* of the plot, according to the real or binary number in Stack Level 1. For example, if that number is `3.00` or `# 3d`, then AUTO or DRAW will calculate and plot a function value every *third* pixel column in a FUNCTION plot. The programmable version of → **RES** would be   « PPAR 4 GET
                                                                »

Related to RES is system flag –31, the "Curve filling" ("dot-connecting") flag: When flag –31 is clear, curve filling is enabled; the 48 will connect each consecutive pair of plotted points with a straight line. But when you set flag –31, curve filling is disabled. So using RES and Flag –31 can save you a lot of computation time. Notice that Flag –31 can be set/cleared directly in the MODES menu—with the **CNCT** toggle.

AXES sets the coordinates where the drawn axes will intersect. A single complex number is used as the argument. A programmable version of →**AXES** would be

```
« PPAR 5 GET
»
```

The 48 gives you three different ways to independently specify values for x_{min}, y_{min}, x_{max} and y_{max}:
- **CENT SCALE**
- **XRNG YRNG**
- **PMIN PMAX**

The **CENT SCALE** (CENTR and SCALE) combination is most useful for specifying a certain point to be the center of the plot and then scaling the x- and y- axes relative to each other—as for a polar or conic plot.

CENTR takes a complex number—the center point—as its argument. SCALE takes two real-number arguments: The x-axis scale and the y-axis scale—both in units *per ten pixels*. Thus if (0, 0) is the center of your 131×64 grob, and your x-axis scale is, say, 5, then your grob's x_{min} will be (−130÷2)×(5÷10) or −32.5, and its x_{max} will be 32.5.

A programmable →**CENT** would be

```
« PPAR OBJ→ 6 DROPN
   + 2 /
»
```

A programmable →**SCALE** would be

```
« PPAR OBJ→ 6 DROPN
   SWAP - 10 * C→R PICT
   SIZE 1 - B→R ROT SWAP /
   ROT ROT B→R 1 - / SWAP
»
```

The more rectangular **XRNG**-**YRNG** combination is the most intuitive for FUNCTION type plots and general drawing.

XRNG and **YRNG** are identical in function, taking two real number arguments. The first argument is the minimum range value x_{min}; the second number is the maximum range value x_{max}. XRNG and YRNG are programmable, and programmable versions of their ⇨'ed functions would be:

<table>
<tr><td>

```
« PPAR 1 GET RE
  PPAR 2 GET RE
»
```
</td><td>for x_{min}, x_{max}</td></tr>
</table>

and
<table>
<tr><td>

```
« PPAR 1 GET IM
  PPAR 2 GET IM
»
```
</td><td>for y_{min}, y_{max}</td></tr>
</table>

PMIN and PMAX aren't even mentioned in the Owner's Manual, except in the Operation Index after all the appendices. To use these two commands, you must key them in (or assign them to the Custom keyboard or user keys). Apparently, they were used to set the display limits on the HP-28, and are included in the 48 for compatibility purposes. Of course, the 48 stores these sorts of display limits in PPAR—as the complex numbers PMIN and PMAX. PMIN defines the lower-left corner (x_{min}, y_{min}) of the graphics display, and PMAX defines the upper-right corner (x_{max}, y_{max}). Since PMIN and PMAX are not in a menu, they don't really have ⇨ recall capability, but you can see that the programmable ⇨-equivalents could be:

```
« PPAR 1 GET
»
```
for PMIN

and
```
« PPAR 2 GET
»
```
for PMAX

The last 3 keys in the PLOTR menu let you manipulate PICT size and display limits:

PDIM is a powerful function that allows you to reDIMension PICT. It can affect PICT and PPAR in different ways—best explained on pages 325-326 of the Owner's Manual.

██ ❚H ██ and ██ ❚W ██ are the only programmable "ZOOM" commands in the 48. Both *H and *W *leave PICT unchanged*, but they multiply the height or width, respectively, by an argument. An argument greater than 1 "zooms out," showing more range with less detail; an argument less than 1 "zooms in", showing less range but more detail.

Be careful with *H and *W! Because PICT remains unchanged, it's possible to get plots with different scales superimposed on each other. For example, here's what happens when *W is used carelessly:

```
« ERASE 'Y=SIN(X)'
  STEQ RAD DRAW 2
  *W DRAW 2 *W DRAW
»
```

So to avoid serious trouble, it's a good idea to always follow a *H or *W command with ERASE.

The [PRG]-[DSPL] Menu

Most of the programmable graphics functions you'll use are in the [PRG]-[DSPL] menu. Here they are, listed by menu page:

PICT	PVIEW	LINE	TLINE	BOX	ARC
PIXON	PIXOF	PIX?	PX→C	C→PX	SIZE
→GRO	BLAN	GOR	GXOR	REPL	SUB
→LCD	LCD→	CLLCD	DISP	FREEZ	TEXT

Again, examine these briefly—in related groups:

The commands BOX, LINE and TLINE require two arguments for end-points or diagonal corners. Results are identical to those achieved with the BOX, LINE and TLINE in the interactive graphics environment.

You can express the points either in user units—via complex numbers: (-1.35, 20.6)—as a CAD system does; or as decimal integers representing the pixel column and row: { # 31d # 55d }. In either case, the first term represents the x-axis and the second term the y-axis. The top left pixel of a grob is always { # 0d # 0d }.

The commands C→PX and PX→C allow you to convert between the two, *according to the current values of PPAR.* Remember that each directory will have its own PPAR and its own unique user units.

While the interactive graphics environment has a CIRCL operation but no ARC, the DSPL menu has an ARC command but no CIRCL (you draw a circle as a 360° arc).

ARC takes four arguments. The first two are the center of rotation (in Stack Level 4) and the radius of the arc (Level 3). The units (user vs. pixel) used for these two arguments must match (note that a radius' user units are *x*-axis units only; you can't get an ellipse instead of a circle—even if you want to). The last two arguments are the starting angle in Level 2, and the ending angle in Level 1. Angles are measured and drawn counterclockwise, with zero pointing to the right:

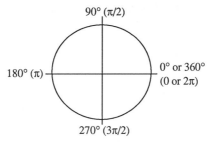

In the interactive graphics environment, **DOT+** and **DOT-** determine whether a pixel will be turned on or off as the cursor lands on it. Pressing one key cancels the other; pressing the same key twice leaves the pixels untouched as the cursor moves around. In programs, use PIXON and PIXOFF to do this. They operate on the pixel located at the coordinates given in Level 1. Again, the pixel may be expressed as a complex number in user units, or as two binary integers in a list.

To test individual pixels, use the **PIX?** command (it returns a 1 if the pixel is turned on; 0 if it's off). And here's a good utility tool, TPIX (Checksum: # 29273d Bytes: 38.5), to toggle any given pixel without having to test it:

```
« DUP
  IF PIX?
  THEN PIXOFF
  ELSE PIXON
  END
»
```

All the grob-building methods mentioned earlier (page 89) are programmable. Three of these live in the (PRG)-**DSPL** menu:

- **→GROB** takes the object in Stack Level 2 and turns it into a grob, using the font size specified in Level 1. The font size specifier is a real number between 0 and 3 and is interpreted as follows:

font size	grob's character height (in pixels)	
3	10	
2	8	
1	6	(characters are all uppercase)
0	10	(for text and numbers), or
	EW	(for algebraics and unit objects)

Try one: Retrieve the T↓oM algebraic from your **G.CH3** directory, then press **0** (PRG) **DSPL** (NXT)(NXT) **→GROB**. You'll briefly see the EquationWriter view of T↓oM before a long grob is returned to Stack Level 1.

- **BLANK** creates a blank grob from width and height arguments given in Levels 2 and 1.

- **LCD→** takes a "snapshot" of the current display and stores it as a grob on the Stack. This is an excellent tool for documenting your applications (note that (STO) serves the same purpose inside the EW and the graphics environment).

Four extremely useful commands allow you to store part of an image as a grob, and to superimpose a small grob on a larger one:

- SUB lets you extract part of a grob (just as you extract part of a list or string object). When used with a grob, SUB takes the grob or PICT from Level 3, and the upper-left and lower-right corners of the area to be SUB'bed from Stack Levels 2 and 1, respectively.

  Try extracting part of the SINE grob: Move to the PICS directory. Press VAR SINE { # 50d # 18d } ENTER { # 85d # 40d } PRG DSPL NXT NXT SUB . You get a 36×23 grob. Press VAR SEE to view it.

- The commands GOR ("Grob OR"), GXOR ("Grob XOR") and REPL ("REPLace") let you *superimpose* one grob upon another. These commands all take the same arguments—the target grob (or PICT), the location, and the grob to be added. The location (Level 2) specifies the spot on the *target grob* (Level 3) where the upper-left corner of the *grob to be added* (Level 1) will go.

  Both GOR and GXOR give a kind of transparency effect thanks to the Boolean logic. GOR will superimpose the pixels of the two grobs in such a way that if *at least* one of the pair of corresponding pixels is "on" then the pixel in the resulting grob is "on." GXOR, on the other hand, will superimpose the pixels so that *exactly* one of the corresponding pair must be "on" in order to turn "on" the pixel in the resulting grob. GXOR, in particular, is useful for manipulating cursors and other kinds of objects that need to always be visible within the background—whether it be dark on light or light on dark.

SUB and **REPL** work here much they work within the *inter-active* graphics environment. Recall that the interactive menu also includes a **DEL** command, to delete or blank out part of a grob, but this isn't in the (PRG)-**DSPL** menu. The best you can do is to create a grob of the right size, using **BLAN**, then **REPL** it onto PICT or the grob.

Three additional commands that control the display that you will find useful in polishing many kinds of programs:

- **CLLCD** simply clears the display. Usually the 48 does it automatically, but sometimes—as with **DISP**—you must do it yourself.

- Use **DISP** to build a *text* display other than the normal Stack display. The display is divided into 7 text lines. **DISP** takes the object from Level 2 and displays it in size-2 font (8 pixels high), on the line specified in Level 1. The upper-most line is numbered 1, the lower-most is numbered 7. **DISP** also honors NEWLINE's ((α)(→)(↵)), so you can get grobs with more than one line of text.

- **FREEZ** keeps parts of the display from updating until some key is pressed. The Level-1 argument is an integer indicating which part(s) to freeze:

1	Status area frozen
2	Stack/Command Line area frozen
3	Status and Stack/Command Line areas frozen
4	Menu area frozen
5	Menu and Status areas frozen
6	Menu and Stack/Command Line areas frozen
7	Entire display frozen

Other Graphics Commands

You can also add grobs with the ⊞ key and invert them with the ⊬⁄₋
key or via the NEG command.

For two grobs of *exactly* the same size, addition goes pixel-by-pixel,
equivalent to: « grob1 { # 0d # 0d }
                          grob2 GOR
                        »

Inverting a grob inverts all the pixels, turning the black ones white and
the white ones black. Just for fun, put the SINE grob onto the Stack.
Then ⊬⁄₋ PICT (STO) and press ◀ to see your creation.

Grobs with row sizes that aren't multiples of eight will be inverted only
insofar as their bits actually represent pixels. For example, GROB 2
2 0000 inverted becomes GROB 2 2 3030. The 3's represent the displayed
pixel pairs, but the 0's are placeholders—bits that don't represent
pixels in the grob.

Use the NEG function to create inverse video effects in your applications. Addition is useful for combining small grobs quickly or "stamp-
ing" frames and legends onto common-sized grobs.

And NEG and ⊞ together can do a GAND ("Grob AND")—the only
Boolean function that HP appears to have omitted. Here's a GAND
program (Checksum: # 61392d   Bytes: 31):   « NEG SWAP
                                              NEG + NEG
                                            »

Store this into your TOOLS directory. Then try it out, using GROB 2 2
3000 and GROB 2 2 1010.   Result: GROB 2 2 1000

Building a Toolbox

With all of its capabilities, the 48 is still missing some useful commands. Such commands are called utilities, and now you're going to create them yourself—along with some "standard" grobs for use in testing/troubleshooting programs. You've already created the SEE utility (in your TOOLS directory), to "view" a grob on the Stack. Also, you have PVUE to avoid the PVIEW bug, TPIX to toggle pixels, GAND for Boolean addition, and GSIZE and $SIZE for memory management.

How about a pair of utilities to store/recall grobs from/to the graphics display? Suppose you create a gorgeous picture—how *do* you save it? Exit to the Stack display, put the name 'GORGEOUS' on Level 1, and use a program, named STOPIC (<u>Checksum</u>: # 49324d <u>Bytes</u>: 30.5):

```
« PICT RCL SWAP STO
»
```

The grob goes onto the Stack and is then SWAP'ped to bring the name to Level 1. Then the grob is stored and the Stack is left as before. Put STOPIC into your TOOLS directory.

RCLPIC does the opposite, taking an object name from Stack Level 1 and (only if it's a grob) storing it into the graphics display. As RCLPIC avoids using GRAPH and PVIEW, it's very general and programmable:

```
« DUP
  IF VTYPE 11 SAME
  THEN RCL PICT STO
  ELSE →STR
    "not a GROB!"
    + DOERR
  END
»
```

RCLPIC (<u>Checksum</u>: # 54937d <u>Bytes</u>: 89.5) chastises you if the named object isn't a grob. Store it alongside STOPIC, in your TOOLS directory.

Now you need to create three empty grobs (change to the **PICS** directory now, to stored them there). Create a 200×200 grob called BIG; a 131×64 grob called NORMAL; and a 2×2 grob called TINY, as follows:

For each grob, put the number of columns (# 200d, # 131d or # 2d) onto Stack Level 2; the number of rows (# 200d, # 64d or # 2d) onto Level 1, and select **BLANK** from the PRG-**DSPL** menu. Then type the name ('BIG', 'NORMAL' or 'TINY') into the Command Line and press STO.

Next, create two non-empty grobs:

First, load the Stack with any four objects, then store the Stack display as a grob, by pressing PRG **DSPL** ◁ PREV **LCD→** NXT 'DISPLAY' STO.

Second, type GROB 5 8 4040E0E0F1F14040 ENTER 'ARROW' STO, to build and store an "arrowhead" grob.

With these 5 good grobs to work with, switch to the **TOOLS** directory to create a custom menu. This custom menu is defined in a list inside a program (feel free to modify the list to serve your own needs):

```
« { PICT BLANK
     ERASE →LCD LCD→
     →GROB SEE STOPIC
     RCLPIC }
  MENU
»
```

Store this menu-building program called GRAFX (Checksum: # 56853d Bytes: 67.5) in your **TOOLS** directory.

Sines and Big Sines

In chapter 4, you used a sine wave to illustrate some of the graphics
capabilities of the 48. Go back now and repeat the exercise on page 84
(don't forget to use RADians mode).... Then store this plot in a grob
called SINE (type [ATTN] 'SINE' [ENTER] STOPIC).

Now create a sine wave plot using the BIG grob: Make sure you're in
the PICS directory. Put the name 'BIG' on Level 1 and execute RCLPIC.
Press [→][PLOT], and be sure the current equation is 'Y=SIN(X)'. Then
set XRNG to (-10, 10) and YRNG to (-1.1, 1.1) (do *not* press **AUTO**—
that would reset XRNG and YRNG). Now just press **DRAW** to draw the
plot... (cookie time).

When the plot finishes, press **LABEL** to add the finishing touches, and
then have a look at this monster. With the graphics menu displayed,
the arrow keys have the following functions:

1. Unshifted arrow keys move the cursor within the display "window." At the edge of the window, they scroll the display across
   the grob—to its actual edge.

2. [→]'ed arrow keys jump the cursor to the edge of the window. At
   the edge of the window, [→]'ed arrow keys jump the cursor and
   display to the edge of the grob.

3. [←][◄] puts you in scrolling mode. Think of scrolling as viewing a
   large picture through a small window or frame: You don't move
   the picture, you move the window.

Press ⬅️◀ now, to get into scrolling mode. In scrolling mode, no cursor is visible, and the arrow keys have the following functions:

1. Unshifted arrow keys scroll the display across the grob.

2. ➡️ed arrow keys jump the display to the edge of the grob.

3. ⬅️◀ returns you to the interactive graphics environment.

Press ATTN to return to the Stack display. Then, in the **PICS** directory, enter the name **'BIGSINE'** onto Level 1 and execute **STOPIC**.

Now you can review both **SINE** and **BIGSINE** any time you want—and you can also practice with other graphics functions on these grobs.

Review

In this chapter, you explored the graphics commands in several of the 48's built-in menus. Then you began to augment those commands with your own graphics "toolbox"—a collection of programs and sample grobs useful in your own graphics development work.

At this point, then, you should have these programs in **TOOLS** (PURGE the object called **TEMP** from **TOOLS** and/or from PICT, if it's still there):

GRAFX	builds a custom menu to make graphics work easier.
RCLPIC	recalls a grob to the graphics display.
STOPIC	stores the graphics display in a grob.
GAND	does a pixel-by-pixel "AND" of two grobs.
TPIX	toggles individual pixels on and off.
PVUE	avoids the 48's PVIEW bug.
$SIZE	finds the byte-size of a grob's string representation.
GSIZE	finds the size of a grob, in bytes.
SEE	graphically displays the contents of a grob.

And you should have these grobs in **PICS**:

BIGSINE	a 200×200 sine-wave plot, with axes
ARROW	a 5×8 arrowhead
DISPLAY	a 64×131 "snapshot" of the Stack display
TINY	a blank 2×2 grob
NORMAL	a blank 64×131 grob
BIG	a blank 200×200 grob
EMPTY	a blank 64×131 grob
SINE	a 64×131 sine-wave plot, with axes

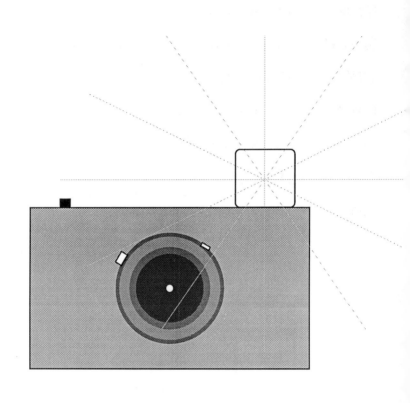

6: GRAPHICS IMPROVEMENTS

Opening Remarks

The PLOT routines give accurate graphical representations of your functions or statistical data. Still, a plot like the one below doesn't tell you much except the shape of the function. For example, you can't tell what the 3 roots of the function are—and you may not even recognize the function.

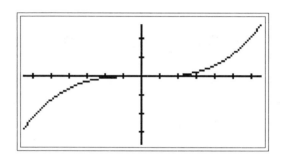

But the 48 does have a command to give the plot some scale—and then you can write a program to add text onto the plot anywhere you wish. You're going to do that here.

Also, you'll be learning how to use the BOX, LINE, TLINE and CIRCLE commands to make your plots more informative.

Labelling the Axes

If you've already tried axis labels, you probably got results like these:

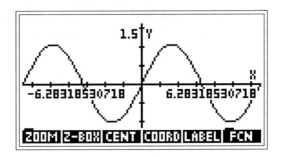

The axis label format uses the current numeric display format. So an
x-axis label of 2π might be plotted in the following ways, depending on
your current numeric display format:

STD	6.28318530718
FIX 4	6.2832
SCI 1	6.3E0

Here's a simple exercise to try the different label formats.

1. Type `'SINE' RCLPIC` to put your SINE grob into the graphics
   display.

2. Press ⟵◀ (or ⟵GRAPH).

3. Press **LABEL**. You should see a picture like the one above.

4. Press ATTN, then ⟵MODES. Change the numeric format to, say,
   FIX 4 or SCI 1. Then repeat steps 1-3 to see how the labels change.

This technique also works with BIGSINE and other oversized plots.

Connecting the Dots

Often, on a graph of a function or statistical data, all the data points are connected by a straight line. This can be a misleading, distracting or just-plain-wrong interpolation of the data. Therefore, the 48 lets you choose plotting with or without lines connecting the data, by setting ⟨☝⟩(MODES)(NXT) **CNCT** (system Flag –31).

To compare, do an AUTO plot of the function 'Y=SIN(X)' with **CNCT** option enabled and then disabled. You should see these plots:

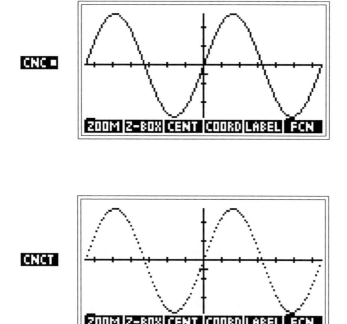

Adding Text to Graphics

Suppose you have a 200×200 grob with a multifunction plot on it and you want to include the names of the three functions being plotted. There isn't a built- in function for adding that text.

You can use the cursor control keys with **DOT+** and **DOT−** to draw the individual letters, but that's tedious—and there's a better way.

Create a new command (call it GLABEL) that places text into the graphics display (or into PICT), with the upper left corner of the text at the coordinates specified. Like most 48 graphics functions, GLABEL should allow you to specify the coordinates either in user units or in pixels. Also, you should be able to specify a font size for the text: 1, 2 or 3 will select small, medium or large text; 0 will select either large text or special formatting (textbook or matrix format), whichever is applicable. Here's a Stack diagram for GLABEL:

Stack Inputs	Stack Outputs
3: Location { # *col* # *row* } or (*x*, *y*)	
2: text string to be placed	(None)
1: Text size (0, 1, 2 or 3)	

And here is GLABEL (<u>Checksum</u>: # 25260d   <u>Bytes</u>: 33):

```
« →GROB PICT 3
  ROLLD GOR
»
```

Store a copy of GLABEL in your **TOOLS** directory.

Now make two variations of GLABEL.

Name the first variation GL↓ (Checksum: # 60923d Bytes: 115.5):

```
« →GROB DUP2 PICT
  ROT ROT GOR SWAP
  DUP TYPE SWAP
  IFERR C→PX
  THEN
  END
  OBJ→ DROP 4 ROLL
  SIZE # 2d + SWAP
  DROP + 2 →LIST
  IF SWAP 1 SAME
  THEN PX→C
  END
»
```

GL↓ puts a label into the graphics display and then returns the location two pixels below the lower left corner of the grob. This will help when you want to create blocks of left-justified text of varying sizes in your graphics display.

Store GL↓ into the TOOLS directory.

Name the second variation GL→ (Checksum: # 57747d Bytes: 172):

```
« →GROB SWAP DUP
  TYPE SWAP
  IFERR C→PX
  THEN
  END
  ROT DUP2 SIZE NEG
  # 10d + # 0d SWAP
  2 →LIST ROT ADDB
  PICT SWAP 4 ROLL
  GOR # 2d + # 0d 2
  →LIST ADDB
  IF SWAP 1 SAME
  THEN PX→C
  END
»
```

GL→ puts a label into the graphics display, and then returns a location two pixels to the right of the upper right corner of the grob. This will help when you want to create a line of various-sized text in the graphics display.

Store GL→ into the TOOLS directory.

Note that before you can use GL→ you must write the small utility it uses: ADDB adds two pixel locations as binary integers.

Here are the Stack diagram and program listing for ADDB:

<u>Stack Inputs</u>   <u>Stack Outputs</u>

2: *location* { # *col₂* # *row₂* }
1: *location* { # *col₁* # *row₁* }   1: *new location*
                                                  { # *col₁*+# *col₂* # *row₁*+# *row₂* }

And here is ADDB (<u>Checksum</u>: # 18393d   <u>Bytes</u>: 51)—store it into your TOOLS directory:

```
« OBJ→ DROP ROT
  OBJ→ DROP ROT
  + ROT ROT +
  SWAP 2 →LIST
»
```

Now look at GL→ once again.

Note that it aligns the *bottom* edges of the text in the graphics display.
Since **GOR**, **GXOR** and **REPL** align to the top left corner of the grob,
GL→ must compute the location of the bottom edge as if your text were
a 10-pixel high grob. That is, since your text will end up as a grob of
height 6, 8 or 10 pixels, depending on the font you use, to align the text
correctly, GL→ must account for those differences in height.

As an illustration, first use GLABEL alone to create a line of text in the
graphics display, using all three fonts. To better see what happens,
incorporate all the commands into a program and EVAL it from the Stack.

```
« { # 0d # 0d } PVIEW
  { # 0d # 0d } "TEXT1"
  1 GLABEL                    (for the first line)
  { # 22d # 0d } "TEXT2"
  2 GLABEL                    (for the second line)
  { # 54d # 0d } "TEXT3"
  3 GLABEL                    (for the third line)
»
```

You'll see three different sizes of text, aligned at the top edges, like this:

TEXT1TEXT2TEXT3

But NOBODYWRITESlikeTHIS. It'sTOOhardtoREAD.

The largest text font on the 48 (not counting equations and unit objects) creates grobs that are 10 pixels high. The command sequence

```
« ... SIZE NEG
   # 10d + ...
»
```

adjusts the placement of text grobs of any size such that all the text ends up aligned at the bottom edges.

Now, erase the display, and then use GL→ to create a line of text like the one you created above, and see the difference. Again, to see it happen, put all the commands in a program and (EVAL) it from the Stack.

```
« { # 0d # 0d } PVIEW
   { # 0d # 0d } "TEXT1" 1 GL→    (for the first line)
   "TEXT2" 2 GL→                  (for the second line)
   "TEXT3" 3 GL→                  (for the third line)
»
```

You'll get the following effect. Notice how the text is aligned on the bottom edge:

TEXT1 TEXT2 TEXT3

Now test GLABEL itself:

Move back to PICS. Put BIGSINE into the graphics display (type 'BIGSINE' RCLPIC). Then →PLOT 6 · 5 +/– SPC 6 · 5 XRNG and 1 · 3 +/– SPC 1 YRNG sets the correct ranges. Then type (.5, 1) "Sine Wave Plot" 3 ENTER GLABEL ENTER, and press ◄ to see your creation (use the arrow keys to scan around until you see this display):

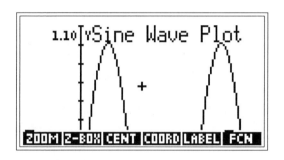

Now put { # 120d # 15d } onto Stack Level 3, your name in quotes onto Level 2 and the number 2 onto Level 1. Execute GLABEL, then ◄. You should see:

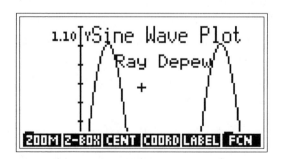

Now put (0.35, 0.5) onto Level 3, "August 1, 1990" onto Level 2, and the number 1 onto Level 1. Execute GLABEL, then press ◀.... You should see the date in 6-pixel text below your name, like this:*

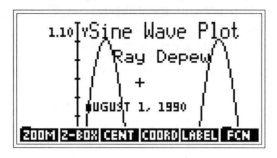

Save this as BIGSINE (in PICS) again (remember how—page 119?).

Now try this: ATTN →PLOT NXT RESET creates a blank 131×64 grob. Then type ←UP { # 1d # 2d } "Welcome" 3 VAR GL↓. You should see { # 1d # 14d }. Now press ◀ to see Welcome in the graphics display. Next, type ATTN "to the new" 2 GL↓ "HP-48SX" 3 GL↓ "Scientific Expandable calculator" 1 GLAB —and press ◀ to see your creation—a startup screen (more on this in chapter 7)!

Best of all, GLABEL, GL→ and GL↓ can be used as subprograms in your own programs, and they can be easily rewritten as functions—or into functions. They don't halt program execution, and they're not interactive; they take their arguments from the Stack. They're also fairly tidy: they clean up the Stack after themselves. However, they do alter PICT irreversibly, and they don't include error checking—they assume you have given them correct inputs.

---

*WARNING: If you execute GLABEL from your TOOLS directory, you may get different results from those pictured here. GOR and other graphics commands compute user units as specified by PPAR *in the current directory*. If your directories have PPAR's with differing user units, your results will be unpredictable. Therefore, it may be advisable to avoid user units in cases like this.

Here's one more handy routine, called CTR, that centers text around a given point in a grob. The text is drawn in font size 1:

CTR

Checksum: **# 63567d**
Bytes: **60**

Stack Inputs   Stack Outputs

3: *target* GROB *(may even be PICT)*
2: *location* { **#** *row no.* **#** *column no.* }
1:            "*text*"   1: *modified* GROB

```
« 1 →GROB DUP SIZE
  DROP 2 / ROT EVAL
  SWAP ROT - SWAP 2
  →LIST SWAP GOR
»
```

Store CTR into your **TOOLS** directory. Then test it and experiment with it as you wish.

Adding Graphics to Enhance Plots

Purge PICT and pull out BIGSINE again. Now suppose you want to label the origin. How do you do this?

Press ◄NXT to get to the drawing menu. Then use the arrow keys to position the cursor on (0,0) and press ✕. Press any arrow key four times, then **CIRCL**. Now the origin is circled. Next, press the arrow keys to get the cursor at the 4 o'clock position on the circle. Press ✕ again. Press ▶ *fifteen times*, then ▼ *eight times*, then **TLINE**.

You've now drawn a line from the circle to some arbitrary point. The Toggle LINE function draws a line that turns black pixels white and white ones black. Now press ENTER to save the pixel position to the Stack. Then press ATTN to return to the Stack for a moment.

Back in the Stack display, you see the digitized cursor position on Level 1. You want to label the origin as either ORIGIN or 0.0000 (your choice). With the cursor position on Level 3, put either "ORIGIN" or 0 onto Level 2, and 1 onto Level 1. Then execute GLABEL.* Finally, press ◄.

Move the cursor to just under the 0. Now press ✕, then ▶ repeatedly to move the cursor to the end of the label. Press **LINE** to underline the label (you could also use **DOT+** to do all this, but the canned shape routines are faster in a program and give more predictable results—use them as much as possible).

---

*Remember the hazards of differing PPAR's in different directories (see the footnote on page 132).

Your grob should now look like this.

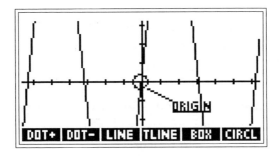

Hmm…in a presentation-quality plot, the title block should probably be enclosed in some kind of box, no?

All right: Press the arrow keys to get the cursor above and to the left of the title, Sine Wave Plot. Press ⊗. Now move the cursor below the date and to the right of the title and your name. Press **BOX**, and you should see your title block as shown below.

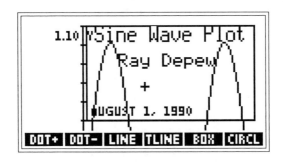

Save this as BIGSINE (in PICS) again.

Review

In this chapter you learned how to manipulate the PLOT functions to display your plot the way *you* want to see it. You learned how to display the axis labels in different numeric formats.

You also created some programs to place text—of various sizes—anywhere on a plot. These programs, GLABEL, GL↓, GL→ and ADDB, are important additions to your toolbox.

You then used some of the *shape* commands (e.g. **BOX**, **CIRCL**, **LINE**, **TLINE**) to accent your plot. This is what the shape functions were originally intended for.

In fact, from now on, you can refer to the shape commands as "freehand drawing figures." Together with the freehand drawing commands **DOT+**/**PIXON** and **DOT-**/**PIXOF**, they form the core of the 48's tremendous graphics capability. And that's what the next chapter is devoted to—freehand drawing.

Graphite Grobs*

*Notes, doodles, Cookie Art, etc.

7: FREEHAND DRAWING

How to Do It

What if you could turn on your 48, or start a program, and see an opening display like this?

With freehand drawing, you can create graphics to give your programs more pizzazz, simplify and clarify user interaction, or produce more intuitively understandable, pictorial outputs.

This chapter shows you how to do it.

The procedure for creating freehand graphics is this:

1. Use **BLANK** or **ERASE** to create a blank grob—your drawing board.

2. Use **XRNG** and **YRNG**, or **PDIM**—or even **CENT** and **SCALE**—to define your user units. Or, just work in pixels.

3. Use **BOX** to draw a single- or double-line around your grob.

4. Use **LINE** , **CIRCL** , etc. as much as possible, and **PIXON** / **DOT+** , **PIXOF** / **DOT-** only when the shapes won't do. In the Welcome picture at the start of the chapter, for example, all parts of the calculator except the keys were drawn with **LINE** and **ARC** . The keys were **DOT+** work. The text was done with GL↓ and GLABEL.

5. Periodically during your creation (and of course, when it's done), save your drawing by typing 'TITLE' (or any other name), then STOPIC. Remember that your grob is only an object, which can be lost with a single keystroke.

Now use this program, named OFF1 (store it in your **HOME** directory: Checksum: # 38534d Bytes: 68):

```
« { HOME TOOLS PICS TITLE }
  RCL PICT STO OFF
  { } PVIEW
»
```

You can add it to your CUSTOM menu, or assign the program to the ⤷OFF key. Then, whenever you use OFF1 to turn the calculator off, you'll see your own TITLE grob.*

---

*With everything else the 48 has, it's a pity HP didn't include (or at least document) an AUTOSTART feature—a flag to activate a user program whenever the machine is turned on.

Drawing a Voltmeter Face

As another example, here's how to use freehand drawing figures and user units to create the face of an analog instrument meter, such as a voltmeter. You should end up with a grob that looks like this:

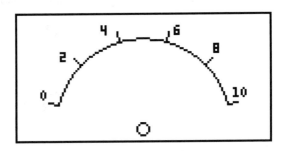

Press ⟨→⟩⟨PLOT⟩⟨NXT⟩ **RESET** to create a blank 131×64 grob. Then press ⟨◀⟩ to get to the graphics environment, and put a frame around the grob by drawing a box: ⟨→⟩⟨◀⟩⟨→⟩⟨▲⟩ ⟨✕⟩⟨→⟩⟨▶⟩⟨→⟩⟨▼⟩⟨→⟩⟨▼⟩⟨NXT⟩ **BOX** .

Now define your drawing area in user units. To make it easier, call the pivot point of the needle the origin, or (0, 0).

Give the arc on the numeric scale a radius of 0.9 unit from the origin. Then, allowing for tic marks and lettering, your maximum meter height will be 1.14 units, and your minimum meter height will be –0.12 units. For now, use a meter width of 2.6 units.

Note that you are using arbitrary units right now. When creating a strip chart or a bar graph, you'll probably want to use more meaningful units, like dollars/month or thousands of barrels per day, etc.

You can set your user units in two ways:

- Specify the lower-left and upper-right corners via PMIN and PMAX:
  (-1.3,-.12) PMIN (1.3,1.14) PMAX (ENTER)

- Or, specify the *x*- and *y*- ranges, using **XRNG** and **YRNG**:

  -1.3 1.3 **XRNG** -.12 1.14 **YRNG**

Either approach works fine. What you're doing is setting the plotting limits in terms of your own units. This diagram illustrates the relationship between PMIN / PMAX and **XRNG** / **YRNG**:

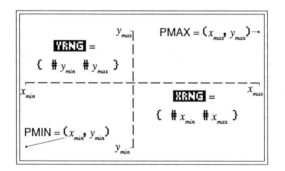

Now draw a small circle at the pivot point. You can do this from the Stack or from the GRAPHICS environment.

From the graphics environment, use **COORD** to find the pixel closest to (0,0), then ⊠▶▶▶ (maybe ⊟ to get the menu back), then [NXT] **CIRCL**.

Or, to draw the pivot circle from the Stack, place these arguments on the Stack:

4:	(0, 0)	center of the circle
3:	.03	radius of the circle
2:	0	start angle of the circle
1:	360 or 6.2832	end angle of circle (° or rad)

Then press [PRG] **DSPL** **ARC** (the **CIRCL** command doesn't work on the Stack, and **ARC** doesn't work in the graphics environment.)

Next, draw the meter arc, by using [PRG] **DSPL** **ARC**, with these Stack arguments:

4:	(0, 0)	center of the arc
3:	0.9	radius of the arc
2:	15 or 0.2618	arc start angle ($\pi/8$ RADians)
1:	165 or 2.8798	arc end angle ($7\pi/8$ RADians)

Now draw the 6 tic marks in the graphics environment, by "eyeballing" their locations (you could calculate their locations exactly, but you'll get equally good resolution using the interactive commands): Move the cursor to the point on the arc where the tic mark originates; press ⊠. Then move the cursor to the other end of the tic mark, and press **LINE**. Repeat this for all six tic marks, evenly spaced.

Now use the GLABEL utility from Chapter 6 to label the tic marks. You want to label the tic marks 0, 2, 4, 6, 8 and 10.

For each label, follow this procedure:

1. Press ←GRAPH or ◄ to get the graphics environment. Move the cursor to the point above the tic mark where the label belongs, and press ENTER.

2. Press ATTN to exit graphics. Put the label on Level 1 as a string, i.e. "0", "2", "4", etc. Press 1, then execute GLABEL.*

At the end, your grob should look like the figure shown on page 141. Store this grob by entering 'METER' STOPIC.

Later, you will see how this versatile grob can be used in conjunction with the RS-232C interface to simulate a wide variety of measurement instruments.

---

*Keep in mind that GOR, GXOR and REPL use the plotting limits in the current directory when they add data to PICT. This can give you unexpected results if you execute GLABEL from a directory with a different PPAR than what you intend.

Review

In this chapter you've seen the freehand drawing tools and a few examples for using them to create your own grobs, not necessarily tied to the normal PLOT routines. You should feel free to explore any other uses for grobs you can think of.

Keep in mind that a freehand grob can also be created programmatically, by using the commands from within ≪ ≫. Or, you can use RCLPIC to recall the (previously stored) grob, or SEE if the grob is on the Stack. And any grob on the Stack can be turned into a program by placing it on the Command Line and enclosing it in ≪ ≫ brackets.

Now you're ready to see some real applications—examples of how you might put together everything you've learned here so far....

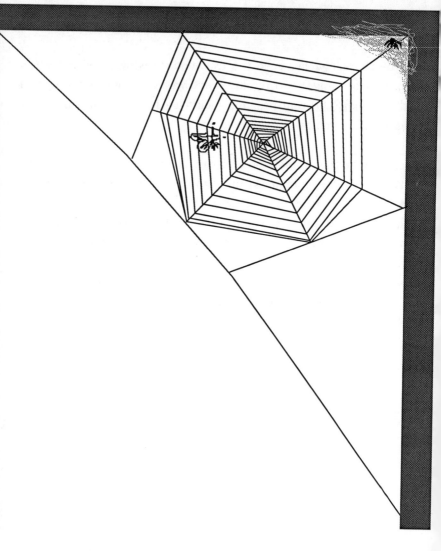

8: Programmable Graphics

Applications

Introduction

In this chapter you're going to see several graphics applications. Some are meant to be used "as is," while others are given simply as examples of what you can do with graphics—to be modified or finished to fit your needs.

Each application begins with a description of the program(s). Then follows a list of subroutines and other variables, then a complete set of program listings, along with checksums, byte counts, Stack argument listings (where appropriate), notes and/or comments (where appropriate). Occasionally, too, you may see multiple versions of a program—just to show you how different your approaches can be.

*The checksum and byte counts given are for a Rev. A machine. To compare checksum and byte count, enter the program and store it under the indicated name. Then put that name onto Stack Level 1 and press ←[MEMORY] BYTES.

Programmable Scanning Inside a Big Grob

These programs automate scanning inside a large grob—say, 300×200.

Descriptions

PSCAN: To display only certain, predetermined parts of the grob, you can use PSCAN from within a program to display those parts.

SCAN: To examine the grob yourself, use SCAN as a versatile alternative to the built-in GRAPHICS scrolling mode, moving by pixel, ten pixels, or across the entire grob.* SCAN treats the 48 display as a window onto the grob and redefines the numeric keypad as a window control pad; each numeric key, except 5 and 0, indicates a direction for movement:

- The 7 key, for example, moves the grob *one pixel* up and to the left (that is, it moves the window one pixel down and to the right).

- ⇐7 moves the grob *ten pixels* up and to the left.

- ⇒7 moves the grob to the upper left corner of the window.

- Similarly, the other numeric keys move the grob in their directions: 3 to the lower right, 6 to the right, etc. (5 does nothing).

- 0 exits SCAN in an orderly fashion. ATTN is OK for emergencies, but it will leave the directory cluttered with extra objects.

---

*You may wish to disable the clock display (clear system flag −40) when using SCAN. A system bug causes the clock display to appear on the top edge of the grob, where it scrolls off- and on-screen, as part of the grob. Interestingly, the clock even keeps "ticking" as it moves around (at least in Rev. A calculators). HP will probably fix this in a later ROM revision.

Subroutines

PSCAN, SCAN and these subroutines should all be in the same directory.

SETUP:	Creates temporary variables and initializes the 48 properly for SCAN and PSCAN.
NUDGE:	"Nudges" the graphics display the distance and direction given in Level 1.
MV1:	Moves 1 pixel in the direction indicated.
MV10:	Moves ten pixels in the direction indicated.
MVall:	Moves across the entire grob, in the direction indicated.
ADDB:	Adds two lists of the form { # *rrr* # *ccc* } (see page 128).
PVUE:	Corrected version of PVIEW (see page 102).

Alternate Approach

These routines offer another solution, for the sake of comparison.

PSCN	An alternate version of PSCAN.
SCN	An alternate version of SCAN.
MV	Combines the functions of NUDGE, MV1, MV10 and MVall above. Moves the distance indicated (1 pixel, 10 pixels or all the way) in the direction indicated.
PVU	An alternate, program-specific version of PVUE.

SCAN

```
« SETUP                              (Initialize PICT and variables)
   Cursor PVIEW
   DO 0 WAIT DUP FP
      → ky kfp
      « CASE
           kfp .1 SAME               (Unshifted)
              THEN ky MV1
              END
           kfp .2 SAME               (⟨←⟩-shifted)
              THEN ky MV10
              END
           kfp .3 SAME               (⟨→⟩-shifted)
              THEN ky MVall
              END
        END
        ky
      »
   UNTIL 92.1 SAME                   (Key zero—exit)
   END
   { Cursor PSIZE } PURGE            (Remove global variables)
»
```

Checksum: # 47364d
Bytes: 257.5

	Stack Arguments	Stack Results
1:	(none)	(none)

Notes: SCAN uses PICT.

PSCAN

```
« OBJ→      (Break down list into locations; use list size as a counter)
  DO DUP 1 + ROLL PVIEW       ("Roll up" to the next location,
     .5 WAIT 1 -                   use it and discard it)
  UNTIL DUP 0 SAME
  END
»
```

Checksum: # 29420d
Bytes: 67.5

Stack Arguments	Stack Results
1: { loc_1 loc_2 loc_3 ... loc_n }	(none)

Notes: PSCAN uses PICT.

The Stack argument may be given either in user units (complex numbers) or pixel locations { #*rownum* #*colnum* }. Each set of coordinates in the list represents a location on the grob that will successively be passed to PVIEW in the program.

SETUP

```
« PICT SIZE DUP2 2 →LIST
   'PSIZE' STO                        (Save PICT size)
   IF # 64d ≤ SWAP         (If PICT is no bigger than the default...
      # 131d ≤ AND
   THEN                     ...offer to view without scrolling or aborting)
      IF "GROB is smaller than■   (■ is NEWLINE; press →←)
         display! Look anyway?"
         { { "YES" « 1 CONT » }
         "" "" "" ""
         { "NO" « 0 CONT » } }
         TMENU PROMPT 0 MENU
      THEN { } PVIEW                  (Press ATTN to exit from this)
      END
      CONT                    (CONT breaks out of SCAN here)
   ELSE { # 0d # 0d }
      'Cursor' STO                    (Initialize the cursor)
   END
»
```

Checksum: # 22047d
Bytes: 311.5

	Stack Arguments	Stack Results
1:	(none)	(none)

Notes: SETUP initializes SCAN and PSCAN.

NUDGE

```
« Cursor ADDB                    (Add increment to Cursor)
  → cursor
  « IFERR cursor PVUE      (PVUE traps the PVIEW bug—see Ch. 5)
    THEN 300 .2 BEEP
     DROP
    ELSE cursor
       'Cursor' STO           (Update Cursor for next time)
    END
  »
»
```

Checksum: # 34653d
Bytes: 148

Stack Arguments   Stack Results

1: { # *column-increment* # *row-increment* }   (none)

Notes: NUDGE moves the grob according to the increment given in Level 1.

The increment must be given in binary integers.

NUDGE is called by MV1 and MV10.

MV1

```
« → ky
  « CASE
      ky 62.1 SAME                      (Key 7, up and left)
          THEN { # 1d # 1d } NUDGE
          END
      ky 63.1 SAME                      (Key 8, straight up)
          THEN { # 0d # 1d } NUDGE
          END
      ky 64.1 SAME                      (Key 9, up and right)
          THEN { #18446744073709551615d # 1d } NUDGE
          END
      ky 72.1 SAME                      (Key 4, left)
          THEN { # 1d # 0d } NUDGE
          END
      ky 73.1 SAME                      (Key 5, nowhere)
          THEN { # 0d # 0d } NUDGE
          END
      ky 74.1 SAME                      (Key 6, right)
          THEN { #18446744073709551615d # 0d } NUDGE
          END
      ky 82.1 SAME                      (Key 1, down and left)
          THEN { # 1d #18446744073709551615d } NUDGE
          END
      ky 83.1 SAME                      (Key 2, straight down)
          THEN { # 0d #18446744073709551615d } NUDGE
          END
      ky 84.1 SAME                      (Key 3, down and right)
          THEN
            { # 18446744073709551615d
              # 18446744073709551615d }
            NUDGE
          END
    END
  »
»
```

<u>Checksum</u>: # 48305d
<u>Bytes</u>: 652.5

	Stack Arguments	Stack Results
1:	*keycode*	(none)

<u>Notes</u>: MV1 moves the grob 1 pixel at a time.

You cannot create the large binary integer in MV1 via # 1d +/−
while editing the program. You'll get « ... # 1d NEG ... »,
which won't work in the program. And # 1 +/− α←D causes
an Invalid Syntax error at « ... # -1d ... ».

To get the large integer, then you must either key it in digit-
by-digit each time (not too thrilling a prospect) or put it onto
the Stack before keying in the program, then pull it into the
program during editing via ←EDIT **↑STK**. This seems far
easier, since the number is just the negative of a smaller, more
familiar integer:

1 ENTER+/−   <u>Result</u>: # 18446744073709551615d

Then, while creating your program, put the insert cursor (♦)
in the space to the right of where you want to place the integer.
Press ←EDIT to get the EDIT menu and **↑STK** to get to the
selection environment. Use ▲ and ▼ to select the integer, and
then **ECHO** ENTER. You'll return to the program editing, with
the integer in the right place.

MV10

```
« → ky
  « CASE
      ky 62.2 SAME                          (Key ←7, up and left)
         THEN { # 10d # 10d } NUDGE
         END
      ky 63.2 SAME                          (Key ←8, straight up)
         THEN { # 0d # 10d } NUDGE
         END
      ky 64.2 SAME                          (Key ←9, up and right)
         THEN { # 18446744073709551606d # 10d } NUDGE
         END
      ky 72.2 SAME                          (Key ←4, left)
         THEN { # 10d # 0d } NUDGE
         END
      ky 73.2 SAME                          (Key ←5, nowhere)
         THEN { # 0d # 0d } NUDGE
         END
      ky 74.2 SAME                          (Key ←6, right)
         THEN { # 18446744073709551606d # 0d } NUDGE
         END
      ky 82.2 SAME                          (Key ←1, down and left)
         THEN { # 10d # 18446744073709551606d } NUDGE
         END
      ky 83.2 SAME                          (Key ←2, straight down)
         THEN { # 0d # 18446744073709551606d } NUDGE
         END
      ky 84.2 SAME                          (Key ←3, down and right)
         THEN
            { # 18446744073709551606d
              # 18446744073709551606d }
            NUDGE
         END
   END
  »
»
```

<u>Checksum</u>: # 38008d
<u>Bytes</u>: 653.5

	<u>Stack Arguments</u>	<u>Stack Results</u>
1:	*keycode*	(none)

<u>Notes</u>: MV10 moves the grob 10 pixels at a time.

As with MV1, to get the large integer here, you must either key it in digit-by-digit each time or put it onto the Stack before keying in the program, then pull it into the program during editing via ←[EDIT] **↑STK**. Again, this seems far easier, since the number is just the negative of a smaller, more familiar integer:

10 [ENTER][+/−]   <u>Result</u>: # 18446744073709551606d

Then, while creating your program, put the insert cursor (♦) in the space to the right of where you want to place the integer. Press ←[EDIT] to get the EDIT menu and **↑STK** to get to the selection environment. Use [▲] and [▼] to select the integer, and then **ECHO** [ENTER]. You'll return to the program editing, with the integer in the right place.

MVall

```
« → ky
  « CASE
      ky 62.3 SAME              (Key →7, up and left)
         THEN PSIZE
            { # 18446744073709551485d
              # 18446744073709551552d }
            ADDB
         END
      ky 63.3 SAME              (Key →8, straight up)
         THEN Cursor OBJ→ DROP2
            PSIZE OBJ→ ROT DROP2
            # 64d - 2 →LIST
         END
      ky 64.3 SAME              (Key →9, up and right)
         THEN # 0d PSIZE OBJ→ ROT
            DROP2 # 64d - 2 →LIST
         END
      ky 72.3 SAME              (Key →4, left)
         THEN PSIZE OBJ→ DROP2
            # 131d - Cursor OBJ→
            ROT DROP2 2 →LIST
         END
      ky 73.3 SAME              (Key →5, nowhere)
         THEN Cursor
         END
      ky 74.3 SAME              (Key →6, right)
         THEN # 0d Cursor OBJ→
            ROT DROP2 2 →LIST
         END
      ky 82.3 SAME              (Key →1, down and left)
         THEN PSIZE OBJ→ DROP2
            # 131d - # 0d 2 →LIST
         END
      ky 83.3 SAME              (Key →2, straight down)
         THEN Cursor OBJ→ DROP2
            # 0d 2 →LIST
         END
```

```
      ky 84.3 SAME                  (Key →3, down and right)
         THEN { # 0d # 0d }
         END
      Cursor                        (If no other case is true)
   END                                                  (CASE)
 »
 DUP 'Cursor' STO PVIEW
»
```

<u>Checksum</u>: # 44757d
<u>Bytes</u>: 674

	Stack Arguments	Stack Results
1:	*keycode*	(none)

Notes: MVall moves the grob all the way to one side or corner.

As with MV1 and MV10, to get the large integers here, you must either key them in digit-by-digit each time or put them onto the Stack before keying in the program, then pull them into the program during editing via ←EDIT **↑STK**. This seems far easier, since the numbers are just the negatives of smaller, more familiar integers:

131 ENTER+/−   <u>Result</u>: # 18446744073709551485d
64 ENTER+/−   <u>Result</u>: # 18446744073709551552d

Then, while creating your program, put the insert cursor (♦) in the space to the right of where you want to place an integer. Then press ←EDIT **↑STK**, and use ▲ and ▼ to select the integer, then **ECHO** ENTER.

Listings for Alternate Approach

Often you may first solve a programming problem in the way clearest
to you, only to discover later that you could have accomplished the
same task more simply, or with less code, less memory usage, better
execution speed, etc. In fact, the very act of creating and documenting
the first version often reveals the possibilities for improvement.

This application is a good example of that process. After studying the
previous version, you'll see how this version "streamlines" it somewhat
(though the effective speed is about the same either way):

PSCN

```
« OBJ→ 1
  FOR j j ROLL
    PVIEW .5 WAIT -1
  STEP
»
```

Checksum: # 12373d
Bytes: 58

Stack Arguments	Stack Results
1: $\{$ loc_1 loc_2 loc_3 ... loc_n $\}$	(none)

Notes: PSCN is very similar to PSCAN (page 151).

SCN

```
« { # 0d # 0d } PVIEW                    (Display PICT)
  RCLF 'Flags' STO 64 STWS      (Save current flag settings
                                 before messing with them)
  PICT SIZE 64 - B→R 'PY' STO      (Re-size PICT if
  131 - B→R 'PX' STO                it's too small)
  0 'CX' STO 0 'CY' STO         (Initialize variables)
  WHILE 0 WAIT DUP 92.1 ≠            (Get keycode)
  REPEAT DUP IP                     (Dissect it into two
    SWAP FP 10 *                   arguments for MV)
    MV PVU           (Do the move and display the result)
  END
  DROP Flags STOF      (Restore previous flag settings)
  {Flags PX PY CX CY } PURGE            (Clean up)
»
```

Checksum: # 40288d
Bytes: 295

	Stack Arguments	Stack Results
1:	(none)	(none)

Notes: SCN behaves like SCAN (page 150).

MV

```
« { 1 10 1E12 } SWAP GET
  → f
  «
    { { 1 1 } { 0 1 } { -1 1 }
      { 1 0 } { 0 0 } { -1 0 }
      { 1 -1 } { 0 -1 } { -1 -1 } }
    { 62 63 64 72 73 74 82 83 84 }
    ROT POS GET EVAL
    f * CY + PY MIN 0 MAX 'CY' STO
    f * CX + PX MIN 0 MAX 'CX' STO
  »
»
```

Checksum: # 57437d
Bytes: 348.5

	Stack Arguments	Stack Results
2:	*keycode (integer portion)*	(none)
1:	*keycode (tenths digit)*	(none)

Notes: MV moves the grob as indicated by the two keycode arguments it receives from SCN. Compare this with NUDGE, MV1, MV10, and MVall on pages 153-159. Note, too, that since only SCN calls MV—and only once—you could certainly incorporate MV into SCN with no loss of efficiency.

PVU

```
« CX R→B CY R→B
  2 →LIST PVIEW
»
```

Checksum: # 24367d
Bytes: 41

	Stack Arguments	Stack Results
1:	(none)	(none)

Notes: PVU is a program-specific version of PVUE (page 102). That is, since the assumption is that PVU is to be used only with SCN, it doesn't do the type-checking that the more generalized PVUE does. Note, too, that since SCN calls PVU only once, you could also incorporate PVU into SCN with no loss of efficiency.

Generating a Stripchart

Here are two programs which allow you to display data in a stripchart format. A stripchart recorder is a mechanism that drags a strip of paper at a constant speed under a pen being activated by a signal from an instrument or sensor. Usually the signal is a 0-5-volt or 4-20-milliamp signal.

Now, with the advent of low-power signal conditioning modules, you can read an analog signal input, then convert it to a real number and transmit it via datacomm lines to a digital computer.*

The 48 has a unique position as a portable instrument controller or data logger: On the last page of the I/O menu are some low-level commands with which you can configure your 48 to communicate with any serial device in the world. These stripchart programs and the ᏙᎷ program which follows, are intended to demonstrate this capability.

*Signal conditioning modules that do this are available from Omega Engineering, DGH and many other sources. Most modern test & measurement instruments are now sold with a built-in or optional serial interface.

Descriptions

STRIP: This program displays an animated (rolling) stripchart on the display. It may be halted by pressing any key.

PSTRIP: This program prints a stripchart on the infrared printer. The output is very elementary, but the program is easily modified to add more detail to the output. It may be halted by pressing any key.

STRIP and PSTRIP do not take their input from the Stack. Instead, they look for a list called DApar ("Data Acquisition parameters"), of the form { *minimum-value maximum-value title time-interval* }, where

minimum-value and *maximum-value* (real numbers) are the chart limits.

title (a character string) is the chart title.

time-interval (a real number) is the minimum interval between measurements (not used in STRIP). This is given in HMS format— as *hh.mmss*, where *hh* is the number of hours, *mm* the minutes, and *ss* the seconds. The routine Nxtime uses this time interval to compute the time until the next measurement. The minimum useful time interval varies from machine to machine, and depends on how long it takes to execute READY and print the results.

If the programs do not find any list object named DApar, then they use this default DApar:

$$\{ \ 0 \ 1 \ "" \ 0 \ \}$$

Note that in a real setting, where the 48 would be connected to a voltmeter or other signal conditioning module, the routine READY would query that instrument or module, and the commands within READY would typically look like this:

```
«   ..."#1RD" XMIT DROP
    REPEAT
    UNTIL BUFLEN DROP
    END
    SRECV DROP ...
»
```

Here, however, for the purposes of these demonstration programs, the input of a real meter is simulated with a random number generator. Therefore READY becomes simply

```
«   RAND
»
```

Subroutines

STRIP and PSTRIP use several subroutines. The main programs and the subroutines should all be stored in the same 48 directory.

READY:	Program to collect the data from the serial- or infrared-equipped sensor or instrument.
MkAxis:	Draws a *y*-axis for PSTRIP paper output.
Now?:	Performs an elapsed-time (true-false) test.
Pr8:	Prints eight pixel rows to the infrared printer.

Variables

DApar:	The data-acquisition parameter list
δt (delta-t):	The time interval, in ticks, between measurements.
Nxtime:	PSTRIP uses a DO...UNTIL loop to time readings, rather than alarms; the current time (in ticks) is incremented by δt to generate the value Nxtime. But in a remote application, PSTRIP could be modified to set alarms and turn itself off, rather than use such a DO...UNTIL loop.

STRIP

```
« RCLF 'Flags' STO 64 STWS          (Save current status)
   IF DApar DUP TYPE 5 ≠            (Find or create DApar)
   THEN { 0 1 "" 0 } DUP ROT STO
   END
   DUP 2 GET SWAP 1 GET DUP2 -      (Extract parameter values
   → hi lo diff                        from DApar)
   « PICT PURGE                     (Draw the stripchart recorder)
     { # 0d # 0d } { # 130d # 63d } BOX
     { # 20d # 11d } { # 120d # 54d } BOX
     20 120
     FOR z z R→B # 55d
       2 →LIST
       PIXON 20
     STEP
     { # 0d # 0d } PVIEW STD       (Show the stripchart recorder)
     PICT { # 20d # 57d }
     lo 1 →GROB GOR                (Label the reticle)
     PICT hi 1 →GROB DUP
     SIZE DROP NEG # 121d + # 57d
     2 →LIST SWAP GOR
     PICT { # 2d # 2d }
     IF DApar 3 GET DUP SIZE NOT   (Draw the title)
     THEN DROP "Press any key to quit."   (Default title)
     END
     1 →GROB GOR
     DO                           (The data acquisition loop)
       READY lo MAX hi MIN lo - diff /
       PICT { # 21d # 12d } { # 119d # 52d } SUB
       PICT { # 21d # 13d } ROT REPL
       PICT { # 21d # 12d } GROB 99
       1 000000000000000000000000 REPL
       100 * 20 + R→B # 12d 2 →LIST PIXON
     UNTIL KEY
     END
```

```
   DROP
 »
 Flags STOF
 { Flags } PURGE
»
```

(Restore status)
(Delete global variables)

Checksum: # 20905d
Bytes: 899

	Stack Arguments	Stack Results
1:	(none)	(none)

Notes: STRIP generates an on-screen stripchart.

DApar may be modified before running the program.

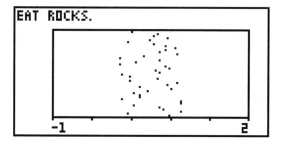

PSTRIP

```
« "Printing Stripchart:" 1 DISP
  IF DApar DUP TYPE 5 ≠              (Find or create DApar)
  THEN { 0 1 "" 0 } DUP ROT STO
  END
  OBJ→ DROP HMS→ 29491200 * 'δt' STO     (Calculate δt)
  DUP
  IF SIZE                           (Print and display the chart title...
  THEN PR1 2 DISP
  ELSE DROP                              ...unless there isn't one)
  END
  DUP2 XRNG -56 7 YRNG        (Set up PICT, draw & print y-axis)
  PICT PURGE
  PICT { # 0d # 0d } MkAxis GOR
  → lo hi
  « TICKS δt + 'Nxtime' STO           (Increment the timer)
    DO 7 0
      FOR rowcounter        (Printer can print 8 rows at once)
        DO
        UNTIL Now?
        END                 (An idle loop: Now? is a T/F test)
        READV                         (Read the "voltage")
        lo MAX hi MIN            ("Peg the meter" limits)
        rowcounter R→C PIXON
        IF rowcounter NOT
        THEN Pr8
        END
        -1
      STEP
    UNTIL KEY
    END                              (End of DO loop)
    "Stripchart completed" 1 DISP Pr8 DROP
  »
  { δt Nxtime } PURGE           (Delete global variables)
»
```

<u>Checksum</u>: # 45726d
<u>Bytes</u>: 472.5

	<u>Stack Arguments</u>	<u>Stack Results</u>
1:	(none)	(none)

<u>Notes</u>: PSTRIP generates a stripchart on the HP 82240A/B infrared printer.

DApar may be modified before running the program.

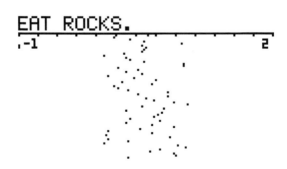

READV

« RAND
»

Checksum: # 51900d
Bytes: 22

	Stack Arguments	Stack Results
1:	(none)	a real number

Notes: READV reads a voltmeter or other serial output device. In this demonstration case, it's a simple random number generator; in real applications, this routine would contain the appropriate commands to read the device.

Now?

```
« TICKS
  IF Nxtime ≥ DUP
  THEN δt 'Nxtime' STO+
  END
»
```

Checksum: # 63658d
Bytes: 70.5

Stack Arguments		Stack Results	
1:	(none)	1	(if it's time to take another measurement, or...)
		0	(...if it's not)

Notes: Now? updates (increments) the value in Nxtime and returns a 1 or 0 to the Stack.

MkAxis

```
« PPAR OBJ→ 6 DROPN                    (Get PMIN, PMAX)
  SWAP RE SWAP IM R→C AXES      (Calculate axis intersection)
  ERASE DRAX LABEL                           (Draw axis)
  PICT { # 0d # 2d }
  GROB 1 6 000000000000 REPL
  PICT { # 0d # 0d }
  { # 130d # 7d } SUB             (Cut out axis for printing)
»
```

Checksum: # 32330d
Bytes: 177

	Stack Arguments	Stack Results
1:	(none)	grob for the y-axis

Notes: MkAxis creates the grob for the y-axis of the stripchart.

Pr8

```
« PICT
   { # 0d # 0d } { # 130d # 7d }
   SUB PR1 DROP ERASE
»
```

Checksum: # 55076d
Bytes: 92

	Stack Arguments	Stack Results
1:	(none)	(none)

Notes: Pr8 sends the top 8 pixel rows of PICT to the printer and then erases PICT.

An Analog Voltmeter

This is a versatile application that lends itself to infinite modification. Using the same DApar and READY as used for the stripcharts, the 48 display becomes an analog meter with a swinging needle. With an analog display, your brain can immediately analyze data without taking the time to translate from digital representation to a quantitative "picture." This is probably why digital car dashboards have disappeared, and the reason for the return of the "old-fashioned" dial—now called "analog" (**Ugh!**)—wristwatch.

Description

The VM application can be used in lieu of the stripchart, when you want instantaneous display of a signal in analog form. VM will draw a voltmeter face in the graphics display, label the display according to the parameters it finds in the list named DApar, and then swing a needle back and forth, using a routine called POINT. The needle's position will reflect the values it receives from the "voltage-reading" routine, READY.

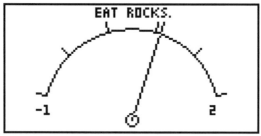

Simply press any key to halt VM. The program and display are simple enough that you can add other features, such as Out of Range indicators, auto-ranging, secondary digital readout, etc.

VM takes no input from the Stack. Instead, it looks for a list called DApar ("Data Acquisition parameters"), of the form { *minimum-value maximum-value title time-interval* }, where

minimum-value and *maximum-value* (real numbers) are the meter limits.

title (a character string) is the meter title.

time-interval (a real number) is the minimum interval between timed measurements (not used in VM).

If the program does not find any list object named DApar, then it uses this default DApar: { 0 1 "" 0 }

Note that in a real setting, where the 48 would be connected to a voltmeter or other signal-conditioning module, the routine READV would query that instrument or module, and the commands within READV would typically look like this:

```
« ... "#1RD" XMIT DROP
  REPEAT
  UNTIL BUFLEN DROP
  END
  SRECV DROP ...
»
```

Here, however, for the purposes of these demonstrations programs, the input of a real meter is simulated with a random number generator. Therefore READV becomes simply   « RAND
                                                                                        »

Subroutines

VM uses the following subroutines, which should be stored in the same directory as VM:

MAKEFACE:	Draws the meter face (if it doesn't already exist), except for the needle, title and scale labels.
READV:	Program to collect the data from the serial device, IR device, or whatever else.
POINT:	Erases and redraws the needle, using TLINE.
CTR:	Centers text around a point in a grob.

Variables

DApar:	The data-acquisition parameter list
MeterFace:	The meter face grob—without needle, titles or scale labels—created by MAKEFACE.

VM

```
« RCLF → f                          (Save current status)
  « -16 SF -19 SF DEG 64 STWS        (Set flags as needed)
    (0,.5) CENTR .2 DUP SCALE        (Set graphics parameters)
    IF DApar TYPE 5 ≠                (Find or create DApar)
    THEN { 0 1 "" 0 } 'DApar' STO
    END
    MAKEFACE PICT                    (Draw the meter face)
    { # 21d # 50d } DApar 1 GET CTR PICT
    { # 104d # 50d } DApar 2 GET CTR PICT
    { # 66d # 2d } DApar 3 GET CTR
    DApar 1 GET DUP POINT            (Put the needle at far left)
    DO READV DUP ROT POINT POINT         (Move the needle)
    UNTIL KEY
    END
    DROP2 f STOF                     (Restore previous status)
  »
»
```

Checksum: # 4616d
Bytes: 417.5

Stack Arguments	Stack Results
1: (none)	(none)

Notes: VM generates a working analog meter in the 48 display. DApar may be modified before running the program.

MAKEFACE

```
« IF MeterFace TYPE 11 ≠
  THEN PICT PURGE
    { # 0d # 0d } PVIEW
    { # 0d # 0d } { # 130d # 63d }
    BOX                              (Meter bezel)
    { # 65d # 57d } DUP
    # 3d 0 360 ARC                   (Needle pivot)
    # 45d 15 165 ARC                 (Scale)
    165 15
    FOR n 1 n →V2 .9 n →V2 LINE -30
    STEP
    PICT RCL 'MeterFace' STO
  ELSE MeterFace PICT STO
    { # 0d # 0d } PVIEW
  END
»
```

Checksum: # 53457d
Bytes: 418.5

	Stack Arguments	Stack Results
1:	(none)	(none)

Notes: MAKEFACE draws the meter face:

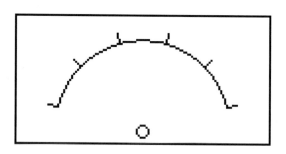

POINT

```
« → ʋ
  « 1
    '15+150*MIN(1,MAX(0,(DApar(2)-
      ʋ)/(DApar(2)-DApar(1))))'
    →NUM →V2 (0,0) TLINE
  »
»
```

<u>Checksum</u>: # 6495d
<u>Bytes</u>: 176

	Stack Arguments	Stack Results
1:	*signal level* (a real number)	(none)

<u>Notes</u>: POINT erases and redraws the meter's needle.

A properly formatted DApar should be in the same directory.

CTR

(see page 133)

READY

(see page 172)

Plots with Two Independent Variables

The 48's built-in plotter allows you to plot multiple equations at once, but it allows only one independent variable at a time.

For example, suppose you have the equation, $'Z=X+Y'$. In order to plot this with both X and Y as independent variables in the 48's built-in PLOT application, you must store several versions of the equation with different values for either X or Y, then create a list containing the names of all the versions of the equation.

That's not as convenient as it could be—with a little help.

Description

MULTIPLOT allows you to plot functions such as $z = f(x,y)$ without all the headache. Before executing MULTIPLOT, you do the following:

1. Create the equation just as you would for the PLOT application; any equation or program that works with PLOT will also work with MULTIPLOT. However, you must store it under a global variable name *other than EQ*.

2. Press →PLOT to get the PLOTR menu. Set up the ranges, independent variable and dependent variable appropriately (see Chapter 5 for a reminder on how to do this—or you can create an entirely new PPAR on the Command Line and store it directly.)

3. Onto Stack Level 1 put a list of this form:

$$\{\ \textit{eqname} \quad \textit{yname} \ \{\ y_1 \quad y_2 \quad ... \quad y_n\ \}\ \}\ \quad \text{where}$$

eqname is the name of the equation (or the equation itself);

yname is the name of the second independent variable;

$y_1, y_2, ...y_n...$ are the values of that variable to be used in the plot.

MULTIPLOT is remarkably small and simple, since it uses built-in 48 routines to do most of the work—and it works at about the same speed as the Plotter application. Some examples follow the program listing.

You may wish to try your multivariable equation with the built-in Plotter first, to find a good range for the second independent variable.

Also, note that you can store and recall the equation lists as desired, effectively saving many different MULTIPLOT applications. And, just as you save lists of single-variable equations as 'varname.EQ', so you might use a standard suffix with two-variable equations—something such as 'varname.MP'.

Variables

VALS: a list of values for the second independent variable

SIV: the second independent variable's current value

MULTIPLOT

```
« 1 GETI STEQ                          (Save equation name in EQ)
  GETI 'SIV' STO GET 'VALS' STO        (Save SIV and VALS)
  ERASE { # 0d # 0d } PVIEW
  DRAX LABEL                           (Draw and label axes)
  1 VALS SIZE
  FOR n                                (For each value ...
    VALS n GET 'SIV' RCL STO           ...store it in 2nd ind. var....
    DRAW                               ...and plot the function)
  NEXT
  { VALS SIV } PURGE                   (Clean up)
  7 FREEZE                             (Freeze the display)
»
```

Checksum: # 18534d
Bytes: 188

	Stack Arguments	Stack Results
1:	{ *eqname yname* { y_1 y_2 ... y_n } }	(none)

Notes: MULTIPLOT generates a plot of the function f(x,y). The function
is plotted in PICT (which is displayed during the plot), and the
program stops with PICT displayed.

Be sure that the PPAR settings are correct.

Example: A Simple Plane

Equation: PLANE: `'Z=X+Y'`

Plot parameters: XRNG: 0 10   YRNG: 0 20
INDEP: X   RES: 0
AXES: (0,0)
PTYPE: FUNCTION
DEPND: Z

PPAR: { (0,0) (10,20) X 0 (0,0) FUNCTION Z }

Level-1 Stack argument: { PLANE Y { 0 2 4 6 8 10 } }

Result: A series of lines representing contours on the plane:

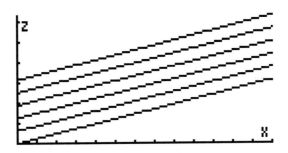

Note that in this example and the next, the dependent variable in PPAR does not appear in the algebraic. This simply allows LABEL to label the _y_-axis correctly and does not affect the computation at all. However, in this first example, the dependent variable in PPAR must be the same as the dependent variable in the equation; an equals sign makes a lot of difference.

Example: A Fourier Series of a Full-Wave Rectified Sine Wave

Equation:　FOURIER: '2*A/π-4*A/π*Σ(n=1,Nmax,
　　　　　　　　　　　　COS(n*ω*t)/(4*n^2-1))'
　　　　　　　(Checksum: # 13515d　Bytes: 120.5)

Variables:　A: 1
　　　　　　　ω: 1

Plot parameters:　XRNG:　0 6.3　　　　YRNG: 0 1
　　　　　　　　　　INDEP:　t　　　　　RES:　0
　　　　　　　　　　AXES:　(0,0)
　　　　　　　　　　PTYPE:　FUNCTION
　　　　　　　　　　DEPND:　f

(PPAR):　{ (0,0) (6.3,1) t 0 (0,0) FUNCTION f }

Level-1 Stack argument:　{ FOURIER Nmax { 1 10 } }

Result: A plot of the first several approximations to the Fourier
　　　　　Series representation of a full-wave rectified sine wave:

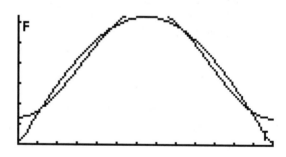

Compare this with a similar plot of the function 'ABS(SIN(ω*t))'. To
see more than one lobe, increase x_{max} from 6.3 to 13 or more.

Example: A Field-Effect Transistor

Equation: IDID0: 'IFTE(VD≤VG-VP,(VD-2/3*(Vbi-VP)*
(((VD+Vbi-VG)/(Vbi-VP))^1.5-
((Vbi-VG)/(Vbi-VP))^1.5))/
(-VP-2/3*(Vbi-VP)*(1-(Vbi/(Vbi-
VP))^1.5)),(1-VG/VP)^2)'
(Checksum: # 60795d   Bytes: 288)

Variables: Vbi: 1
             VP: -2.5

Plot parameters: XRNG: 0 5   YRNG: 0 1
                   INDEP: VD   RES: 0
                   AXES: (0,0)
                   PTYPE: FUNCTION
                   DEPND: ID

(PPAR): { (0,0) (5,1) VD 0 (0,0) FUNCTION ID }

Level-1 Stack arg: { IDID0 VG { 0 -.5 -1 -1.5 -2 } }

Result: A plot of a theoretical ID-VD curve for a FET. The y-axis is
ID/ID_0, where ID_0 is ID at saturation, with zero gate voltage:

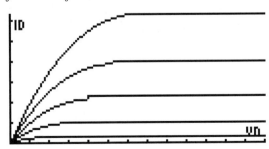

Compare this curve with those found in typical electronics textbooks.

A Contour-Plotting Program

With MULTIPLOT you were introduced to plotting data in three dimensions. But not all three-dimensional data sets can be reduced to a series of equations. Consider, for example, the need to measure current uniformity in a plating tank, or temperature distribution on a heat exchanger fin, or noise levels on a factory floor.

Although such data sets are empirically gathered—not analytically generated—you can nevertheless analyze them with the contour-plot approach by mapping the physical grid of measurements onto an array.

Description

CONTOUR makes a contour plot, taking data contained in an array and displaying it as a three-dimensional surface, as seen from above. The contour lines represent "isovalues"—places on the surface at the same "altitude," or value. An example follows the program listing.

CONTOUR takes all of its arguments from the Stack, including the array of data to be plotted. However, this array will be saved as ARRAY, so that you can modify it after running CONTOUR, if you wish.*

---

*Note that the easiest way to enter array data into the 48 is through the MatrixWriter, ⟨→⟩ MATRIX (for more on the MatrixWriter, read Chapter 20 in the Owner's Manual.)

CONTOUR divides the array into squares, with the points in the array being the corners of the squares:

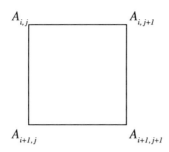

CONTOUR works on one square at a time, cycling through all possible contour values. At each contour value, CONTOUR searches for intersections of the desired contour line with the sides of the square, finding either zero, two or four intersections per square.

If CONTOUR finds zero intersections for a given contour value, it skips to the next value.

If it finds two intersections, it determines which two sides of the square are affected. Simple linear interpolation is used to find the points of intersection, and the contour line segment is drawn in the square.

If it finds four intersections, CONTOUR has encountered a "saddle," where two diagonally opposite corners of the square are higher than the other two corners. Saddles are frequently found in the real world—potato chips, mountain passes, and (of course) a cowboy's saddle.

Saddles are difficult for CONTOUR to draw. It tries to draw a pair of roughly parallel contour lines, closest to the corners whose average value comes closest to the contour value. If the value of the contour is equal to the average of all four corners, then CONTOUR draws two crossing lines in the square.

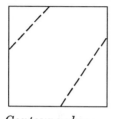 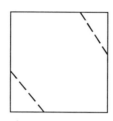 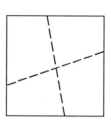

Contour value closest to average of upper-left and lower-right corners *Contour value closest to average of lower-left and upper-right corners* *Contour value equal to average of all four corners*

In each case, simple linear interpolation determines the points of intersection. The more points you have, the more accurate CONTOUR is.

Variables

ARRAY: The name in which the given data array will be saved.

Suggestion: Before keying in CONTOUR, store this list into CST in your TOOLS directory, and then press [CST] to use it as a typing aid:

```
{ ARRAY smallest largest lowlimit hilimit stepsize
  range rows cols ii j ul ur ll lr small big top
  bottom left right contour }
```

CONTOUR

```
« PICT PURGE DUP 'ARRAY' STO
  1 GETI DUP
  → smallest largest    (Local variables for max. and min. values)
  « DO GETI DUP              (Find array's max. and min. values)
      smallest MIN 'smallest' STO
      largest MAX 'largest' STO
    UNTIL -64 FS?C
    END
    DROP2 largest smallest DUP2 -    (Find array's range)
  »
  { # 0d # 0d } PVIEW ARRAY SIZE EVAL
  → lowlimit hilimit stepsize           (Save array
    largest smallest range rows cols     parameters)
  « 1 rows R→C PMIN
    cols 1 R→C PMAX             (Set drawing boundaries)
    1 rows 1 -
    FOR ii                         (For each row...
      1 cols 1 -
      FOR j                       and each column...
        ARRAY ii j 2 →LIST GET         ...work the four cor-
        ARRAY ii j 1 + 2 →LIST GET     ners of the square)
        ARRAY ii 1 + j 2 →LIST GET
        ARRAY ii 1 + j 1 + 2 →LIST GET
        4 DUPN 4 DUPN MIN MIN MIN
        5 ROLLD MAX MAX MAX
        0 0 0 0
        → ul ur ll lr small big
          top bottom left right
        « lowlimit hilimit
          FOR contour              (For each contour value...
            IF 'contour ≥ small      ...if necessary...
               AND contour ≤ big'
            THEN     ...find the number of edge intersections)
              'contour > MIN(ul,ur) AND
               contour < MAX(ul,ur)'
```

```
→NUM 'top' STO
'contour > MIN(ll,lr) AND
   contour < MAX(ll,lr)'
→NUM 'bottom' STO
'contour ≥ MIN(ul,ll) AND
   contour ≤ MAX(ul,ll)'
→NUM 'left' STO
'contour ≥ MIN(ur,lr) AND
   contour ≤ MAX(ur,lr)'
→NUM 'right' STO
'top+bottom+left+right' →NUM
CASE            (How many intersections?)
   DUP 0 ==            (none...
      THEN DROP          ...skip computations)
      END
   DUP 2 ==            (2 intersections)
      THEN DROP
         IF top
         THEN
            'j+(contour-ul)/(ur-ul)'
            →NUM ii R→C
            IF bottom
            THEN            (Top-to-bottom)
            'j+(contour-ll)/(lr-ll)'
               →NUM ii 1 + R→C LINE
            ELSE    (Okay, not top-to-bottom)
               IF left      (Top-to-left?)
               THEN
                  'ii+(contour-ul)/
                     (ll-ul)'
                  →NUM j SWAP R→C LINE
               ELSE    (Aha—top-to-right)
                  'ii+(contour-ur)/
                     (lr-ur)'
                  →NUM j 1 + SWAP
                  R→C LINE
               END
            END      (IF...bottom...ELSE)
         ELSE    (Not top, so try bottom edge)
            IF bottom
            THEN
```

```
                'j+(contour-ll)/
                   (lr-ll)'
                →NUM ii 1 + R→C
                IF left
                THEN           (Bottom-to-left)
                   'ii+(contour-ul)/
                      (ll-ul)'
                   →NUM j SWAP
                   R→C LINE
                ELSE           (Bottom-to-right)
                   'ii+(contour-ur)/
                      (lr-ur)'
                   →NUM j 1 + SWAP
                   R→C LINE
                END
              ELSE     (Not bottom, either, so...
                'ii+(contour-ul)/
                   (ll-ul)'     ...left-to-right)
                →NUM j SWAP R→C
                'ii+(contour-ur)/
                   (lr-ur)'
                →NUM j 1 + SWAP
                R→C LINE
              END        (IF...bottom...ELSE)
            END          (IF...top...ELSE)
          END            (Case of 2 intersections)
      4  ==   (Case of 4 intersections—a saddle—
              so calculate those 4 intersections)
        THEN 'j+(contour-ul)/(ur-ul)'
          →NUM ii R→C
          'j+(contour-ll)/(lr-ll)'
          →NUM ii 1 + R→C
          'ii+(contour-ul)/(ll-ul)'
          →NUM j SWAP R→C
          'ii+(contour-ur)/(lr-ur)'
          →NUM j 1 + SWAP R→C
          'ABS(contour-(ul+lr)/2)'
          →NUM
          'ABS(contour-(ll+ur)/2)'
          →NUM DUP2
```

```
                              IF <        (Diagonal to upper right)
                              THEN DROP2 ROT (Closer to ul, lr)
                              ELSE
                                 IF >     (Diagonal to upper left)
                                 THEN ROT ROT (Closer to ll, ur)
                                 END (So crossover is at midpoint)
                              END                (IF...<...ELSE)
                              LINE LINE
                        END             (Case of 4 intersections)
                  END                                      (CASE)
                END                        (contour range IF test)
                 stepsize
              STEP                        (Next contour value)
           »
        NEXT                                            (For j loop)
      NEXT                                              (For ii loop)
      smallest "Min value" →TAG
      largest "Max value" →TAG
      lowlimit "Min contour" →TAG
      hilimit "Max contour" →TAG
      stepsize "Contour step" →TAG
   »
»
```

Checksum: # 21186d
Bytes: 2420.5

	Stack Arguments	Stack Results
5:		*minimum data value* (tagged)
4:	*low limit* (real)	*maximum data value* (tagged)
3:	*high limit* (real)	*lower contour limit* (tagged)
2:	*step size* (real)	*upper contour limit* (tagged)
1:	*n×m* (real) data array	*contour step size* (tagged)

Notes: Clearly, you could shorten the program with shorter variable names; these were used for clarity. Also, you might explore alternate ways to arrive at the same solution. As you saw with SCAN/PSCAN, there's always more than one way to do things.

Example

With the Stack set up as follows, use CONTOUR to get the result shown:

```
4:   0
3:   5
2:   1
1:   the following array (use the MatrixWriter):
     [[ 0.8 1.3 2.2 0.5 1.3 2.4 1.3 0.5 ]
      [ 0.9 1.5 2.5 0.5 0.9 0.5 0.5 1.5 ]
      [ 1.8 3.0 3.2 1.8 0.5 1.1 2.1 3.0 ]
      [ 1.9 3.2 4.3 1.6 0.8 2.0 2.7 3.3 ]
      [ 1.8 2.1 2.9 1.9 0.5 1.7 2.6 3.7 ]
      [ 1.5 1.4 1.1 0.1 1.5 2.4 2.9 4.0 ]
      [ 1.4 0.9 0.5 1.3 2.1 3.2 3.6 4.2 ]
      [ 1.1 0.9 0.5 1.2 2.8 3.9 4.3 4.8 ]]
```

Drive a Bulldozer Around the Display

This is a fun demonstration of using small grobs as "sprites"—objects that you can move around the display at will.

Description

The main program, called BULLDOZER, uses a list called DOZDATA, which, in turn, consists of two sublists. The first sublist is a list of four grobs, showing the bulldozer facing north, east, south and west. The second sublist is a list of four complex numbers representing those directions. Thus if you tire of the bulldozer image, you can always create another 8×8 grob, then make 3 rotated copies, assemble a new DOZDATA, and run the program with your own custom "sprite."

To start the program, just execute BULLDOZER. A bulldozer will appear at the bottom of the display and start plowing a swath towards the top. Use the arrow keys to control its direction (it will stop when it hits the wall at the edge of the display). Note that these arrow keys are not "north, south, east and west." Rather, they are "forward, reverse, left-turn and right-turn."

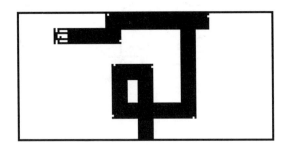

A speed factor is built into BULLDOZER; you change the bulldozer's speed by increasing or decreasing this number. The speed is stored as a local variable in the program, in case you want to add a "gas pedal" key to the program.

Press ENTER to halt the program (if you use ATTN, it may leave a spurious KEY output on the Stack).

Variable

DOZDATA: The grob data for BULLDOZER:

```
{ { GROB 8 8 FFC37EDA5A5A5AFF    (Dozer north)
      GROB 8 8 FB1AFF1D1CFF1AFB    (Dozer east)
      GROB 8 8 FF5A5A5A5B7EC3FF    (Dozer south)
      GROB 8 8 DF58FF38B8FF58DF }  (Dozer west)
    { (0,1) (1,0) (0,-1) (-1,0) } }
```

*(North, East, South and West
in complex numbers)*

(Checksum: # 33345d   Bytes: 172.5)

BULLDOZER

```
« PICT PURGE { # 0d # 0d } PVIEW
  0 131 XRNG 0 63 YRNG (0,0) (131,63) BOX (Define area)
  DOZDATA 1 GET 1 GET (61,8) 1 10 (0,1) RCLF
  → cat locn gear speed direction flags
  « 50 CF PICT locn cat REPL
    DO 'gear*direction+locn' EVAL C→R
      8 MAX 62 MIN SWAP 1 MAX 123 MIN SWAP
      R→C 'locn' STO PICT locn cat REPL
      .3 speed / WAIT
    UNTIL
      IF KEY
      THEN → k
        « CASE
          'k==25'                        (Forward)
            THEN 1 'gear' STO
            END
          'k==35'                        (Reverse)
            THEN -1 'gear' STO
            END
          'k==34'                        (Left turn)
            THEN DOZDATA OBJ→ DROP
              DUP direction POS 1 -
              IF DUP 0 ==                 (You can't turn
              THEN DROP 4                 past 0°)
              END
              SWAP OVER GET
              'direction' STO GET 'cat' STO
            END
          'k==36'                        (Right turn)
            THEN DOZDATA OBJ→ DROP
              DUP direction POS 1 +
              IF DUP 5 ==                 (You can't turn
              THEN DROP 1                 past 360°)
              END
```

```
              SWAP OVER GET
               'direction' STO GET 'cat' STO
          END
        'k==51'
           THEN 50 SF              (Quit)
           END
       END                         (CASE)
     »
   END                             (IF...KEY)
    50 FS?
 END                               (DO...UNTIL)
 flags STOF                        (Clean up)
»
»
```

Checksum: # 6914d
Bytes: 933

Stack Arguments	Stack Results
1: (none)	(none)

Notes: The bulldozer leaves some "litter" when it turns. And different grobs will leave different garbage (the culprits here are the little cutouts behind the dozer's blade). This is because the program turns, increments the position and *then* writes to the display. A commercial game machine would fix this by using a separate sprite for the tracks and/or a "mask" sprite under the bulldozer. But both approaches are slow here and make the dozer flicker. So for this demo, just ignore the litter.*

*But in case you're interested in exploring other solutions here's an observation: A sprite with an all-black border always leaves tracks; if it has an all-white border, it never leaves tracks.

A Friendly Game of Checkers

Here is a checkers game to be played by two 48's—via the Infrared interface or wired serial ports.

This is the book's largest application. If you've been working through Chapter 8 nonstop to this point, **Stop!** Go get some cookies and milk. Give your brain a rest. Then come back.

Description

You start the game by executing CHKRS.

The title screen should appear, with two menu keys to choose **RED** or **BLK** (okay, so it's white and blue—give HP a few more years....)

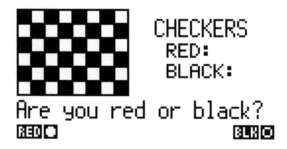

After someone has chosen a color, the other player's color is set, and the 48's set up their playing boards accordingly.

Red moves first, and the two players take turns...

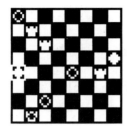

CHECKERS
▶RED:
 BLACK:
YOUR MOVE

...until one player is out of pieces.

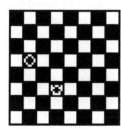

CHECKERS
▶RED:
 BLACK:
WAIT.....

RAD
{ HOME CH.B CHKRS }

4:
3:
2:
1:              "BLACK WINS"
CHKR SETUP REDRA MYMO THMO SELEC

In CHKRS, the numeric keypad becomes a "selector control pad." As with SCAN, the ⑤ key is the neutral center of the pad, and the other non-zero keys act as arrow keys:

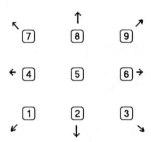

When it's your move, the 48 will highlight a suggested piece to move. Its selections are not very smart, so use the numeric keys to move the highlight to the piece you want to move, and press ENTER. Then press one of the diagonal-move keys (①, ③, ⑤ or ⑦) to indicate the direction you wish to move.

If you choose an invalid move, the piece you selected remains highlighted and you must re-select the move. If it's a valid move or jump, the 48 will update the board display, and send the move information to your opponent's machine. It will also crown your piece if that move sends it to the 8th row.

When your move is over, the 48 passes control to your opponent's machine. At the end of each player's turn, the 48 checks to see if both of you are still in the game, and then goes through the selection and movement procedure again. This cycle continues until one or the other of the players has no more pieces on the board, at which time both machines declare the winner.

The checkerboard layout is contained in an 8×8 array, appropriately called LAYOUT, which is updated during the game to reflect each move. The graphic checkerboard is stored in a grob called BOARD. If you accidentally erase BOARD, don't worry. The STARTUP routine checks for the existence of BOARD, and if it doesn't find it, calls a routine called MAKEBOARD to generate a new one. The pieces themselves are stored as 8×8 grobs called RPIECE, BPIECE, RKING and BKING.

This is indeed a "friendly" game of checkers. A complete and ruthless game would probably require an entire chapter in this book, so this version has the following limitations:

- It won't do multiple jumps (but notice that flag 58 has been left in reserve—for indicating "multiple jump allowed"—so if you're ambitious, go for it).

- The forced-jumping rule is not in effect: If you're in a position to jump, then you are *not* forced to "jump or lose the piece."

- There's no "boss key" to quickly save the current game status as your boss walks up. To abort the game, you must press [ATTN], and risk leaving junk on the Stack.

Subroutines

CHKRS is organized in a modular fashion. This keeps each routine short, easy to understand, and tightly focused.

STARTUP: A routine called initially by CHKRS to check for the existence of a checkerboard grob called BOARD. If it doesn't find BOARD, then STARTUP calls MKBOARD to create one.

STARTUP also prompts the user to choose sides, and waits for input from either the keyboard or the I/O port.

REDRAW: A routine that maps the contents of LAYOUT onto PICT.

MYMOVE: The busiest module in the application, MYMOVE calls SELECT to suggest a piece to play. It accepts key input on the direction to move the piece of your choice, sending this information to a routine called VALID.

VALID: The routine that determines whether your proposed move is legal: You may move only to diagonally adjacent, unoccupied squares, unless you are jumping. You may jump only an opponent in a diagonally adjacent square, and only if the square beyond your opponent's piece is empty. Also, only kings may move or jump backwards.

THMOVE: A routine that waits for an "M", "J", "K" or "D" string from the other machine, then translates the move information and calls MOVEIT to update LAYOUT and PICT. When a "D" is received, THMOVE sets flag 59 and exits.

SELECT: This routine simply searches LAYOUT for the first occurrence of your playing pieces as its suggestion for your next move. Fortunately, it doesn't commit to any square until you press [ENTER] with the square highlighted (The highlight can be on any square—even an empty one or one occupied by an opponent—so if the chosen square is not occupied by one of your pieces, the highlight remains). SELECT will not move past the board edges.

MOVEIT: This routine takes the parameters of the validated move and the piece to be moved and performs the manipulations on LAYOUT and PICT.

MKBOARD: The routine that generates the checkerboard inside a 57×57 grob—called by STARTUP when necessary.

WHOZAT: A small routine that determines which player (if any) is occupying a given square.

C→L: A utility (quite generally useful) that converts a complex number (x, y) into a list of the form { # *row* # *col* }.

GL↓: A text formatting routine (see page 127).

GLABEL: A text formatting routine (see page 126).

Variables

LAYOUT: An 8×8 array listing the entire layout of the checkerboard, created by **STARTUP**. Row 1 of the array is the bottom row of the checkerboard. Element values:

0 = empty 1 = red piece 2 = black piece
3 = red king 4 = black king

Elements on red squares are always zero. Red squares are identified by adding the row and column indices. The sum is always even for red, odd for black.

Initial values (red player's values are shown; exchange 1's and 2's for black players initial values):

```
[[ 0 1 0 1 0 1 0 1 ]
 [ 1 0 1 0 1 0 1 0 ]
 [ 0 1 0 1 0 1 0 1 ]
 [ 0 0 0 0 0 0 0 0 ]
 [ 0 0 0 0 0 0 0 0 ]
 [ 2 0 2 0 2 0 2 0 ]
 [ 0 2 0 2 0 2 0 2 ]
 [ 2 0 2 0 2 0 2 0 ]]
```

Checksum: LAYOUT is dynamic; checksums change.
Bytes: 537.5

BOARD: 57×57 grob of blank checkerboard, created by MKBOARD.
Checksum: #31247d   Bytes: 475.5

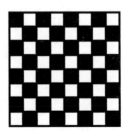

RPIECE: Grob of a red piece: `GROB 8 7 0081C3E7E7C381`

BPIECE: Grob of a black piece: `GROB 8 7 00814224244281`

RKING: Grob of a red king: `GROB 8 7 0000A5E7E7C3C3`

BKING: Grob of a black king: `GROB 8 7 0000A5662442C3`

CHKRS

```
« RCLF 'Flags' STO                    (Save defaults)
  -40 CF                              (Turn off clock display)
  STARTUP REDRAW                (Initialize game, choose sides...
  IF 57 FS?                         ...draw board—red goes first)
  THEN 59 SF                     (Flag 57 set means: "I'm red")
  ELSE 59 CF                    (Flag 59 set means: "My turn")
  END
  DO
    PICT { # 70d # 40d }
    #54 #8 BLANK REPL
    IF 59 FS?                           (My turn?)
    THEN { # 70d # 40d } "YOUR MOVE"
      2 GLABEL MYMOVE
    ELSE { # 70d # 40d } "WAIT....."
      2 GLABEL THMOVE
    END
  UNTIL
    IF LAYOUT →STR DUP "1" POS       (Game ends when...
      SWAP "3" POS OR NOT DUP           reds are gone...
    THEN "BLACK WINS" SWAP
    END
    IF LAYOUT →STR DUP "2" POS       ...or blacks are gone)
      SWAP "4" POS OR NOT DUP
    THEN "RED WINS" SWAP
    END
    OR
  END
  Flags STOF                      (Restore previous states)
  'Flags' PURGE                          (Clean up)
»
```

<u>Checksum</u>: # 19875d
<u>Bytes</u>: 538.5

	<u>Stack Arguments</u>	<u>Stack Results</u>
1:	(none)	"RED WINS"
		or
		"BLACK WINS"

<u>Notes</u>: CHKRS is the main program. Be sure both players have the same I/O setup. This means checking the status of IOPAR, and clearing system flags –33, –34 and –38.

The layout data is stored in the 8×8 array, LAYOUT. Pieces on squares are identified by number:

0 = empty 1 = red piece 2 = black piece
3 = red king 4 = black king

Row 1 in LAYOUT is the first row of the array; Row 1 of the checkerboard is the bottom row of the board—the row nearest you. This makes for faster computing. Notice also that the sum of the row and column numbers of a red square is an even number, while the sum of row and column numbers of a black square is an odd number. This fact speeds up execution time.

Since the game is played only on the black squares, an 8×4 array could also be used. But this would require monitoring of zigzag movements, and the additional code would far outweigh any memory savings from using the smaller array.

All the red squares in the array contain 0's. You could use the red squares for storing game status, etc., if you incorporate a "boss key" into your game, but be aware that some sections of the application check *all* squares for zeros—you can't use the red squares for temporary storage during a game.

These user flags are used:

57   SET: You are red.   CLEAR: You are black.

58   (reserved for use in multiple jumping)

59   SET: Your move.   CLEAR: Their move.

After initialization, CHKRS checks flag 57. Since red always goes first, for the first move CHKRS sets user flag 59 to match flag 57. It then enters a DO...UNTIL loop, which can be exited only when one player runs out of playing pieces (or via (ATTN)). Throughout the game, depending on the status of flag 59, CHKRS calls either MYMOVE or THMOVE ("THeir MOVE").

When it's your opponent's move, the 48 monitors the input buffer for any activity. As soon as some information enters the buffer, the 48 analyzes it and updates LAYOUT and the display.

To communicate between the two machines, the 48 relies on the commands XMIT, BUFLEN and SRECV.

XMIT takes a string from Level 1 and transmits it over the current I/O port. If the transmission is successful, then a 1 is returned to the Stack; otherwise the unsent fragment of the string is put into Level 2, and a 0 into Level 1. Use ERRM to see the cause of the error.

BUFLEN returns the number of characters in the I/O buffer to Level 2 and puts a 1 to Level 1 if no framing errors or UART overruns occur. If an error does occur, then BUFLEN returns the number of characters received before the error to Level 2, and a 0 to Level 1.

SRECV takes the number specified in Level 1, returns that number of characters from the I/O buffer to Level 2, and returns a 1 to Level 1 if the data were retrieved successfully. If an error occurs during SRECV, then Level 2 contains the data received before the error, and Level 1 contains a zero. Execute ERRM to see the cause of the error.

CHKRS does not use the error-trapping capability of these commands, so in order to keep transmission errors to a minimum, CHKRS uses a small number of short messages to communicate between machines. Each message is transmitted as a list inside a string—the most efficient way of passing a variable number of parameters. Valid messages are:

`"{ ` (x_1, y_1) (x_2, y_2) `"M" }"`	Move the piece at (x_1, y_1) to (x_2, y_2).
`"{ ` (x_1, y_1) (x_2, y_2) `"J" }"`	Jump the piece at (x_1, y_1) to (x_2, y_2), capturing the opposing piece en route.
`"{ ` (x, y) `"K" }"`	Crown the piece at (x, y), replacing it with a king of that color.
`"{ "D" }"`	Done. It's the opponent's turn.

The only exception to this "list in a string" rule is the `"R"` or `"B"` that is transmitted at the start of the game, when players are choosing sides.

STARTUP

```
« IF BOARD TYPE 11 ≠                    (Does BOARD already exist?)
  THEN MKBOARD                          (If not, then make it)
  END
  BOARD PICT STO                                  (Draw board)
  (1,-1) PMIN (19.5714285714,8) PMAX    (Set user limits)
  { # 0d # 0d } PVIEW                   (Display board)
  { # 70d # 5d } "CHECKERS" 3 GL↓       (Title labels)
  " RED:" 2 GL↓
  " BLACK:" 2 GLABEL
  PICT RCL                      (Set up prompt to choose color)
  PICT { # 0d # 43d } # 57d # 14d BLANK REPL
  { # 0d # 45d } "Are you red or black?" 3 GLABEL
  PICT { # 0d # 57d }
  GROB 21 7 FFFDF1919D815D55019155015D5501519D81FFFDF1
                                        ("RED" menu key)
  REPL PICT { # 110d # 57d }
  GROB 21 7 FFFDF19D5D815D55719D95715D5571915D81FFFDF1
                                        ("BLACK" menu key)
  REPL
  OPENIO             (Necessary to receive input from the other 48)
  DO
  UNTIL
     IF KEY
     THEN DUP
        CASE
           11 SAME                   (User chooses red....
              THEN DROP "R" "B" XMIT    ... tell opponent)
              END
           16 SAME                   (User chooses black....
              THEN "B" "R" XMIT        ...tell opponent)
              END
           0
        END
     ELSE 0
     END
```

```
    IF BUFLEN DROP DUP          (Opponent chose first)
    THEN SRECV ROT              (What user gets)
    END
    OR  (DO UNTIL loop ends when one of the 3 options is satisfied...
END      ...user chooses red or black, or opponent chooses)
CLOSEIO                         (To save battery life)
SWAP PICT { # 0d # 0d } ROT REPL    (Remove prompt)
IF "R" SAME
THEN 57 SF                                    ("I'm red")
    [[ 0 1 0 1 0 1 0 1 ]              (Red's startup LAYOUT)
    [ 1 0 1 0 1 0 1 0 ]
    [ 0 1 0 1 0 1 0 1 ]
    [ 0 0 0 0 0 0 0 0 ]
    [ 0 0 0 0 0 0 0 0 ]
    [ 2 0 2 0 2 0 2 0 ]
    [ 0 2 0 2 0 2 0 2 ]
    [ 2 0 2 0 2 0 2 0 ]]
    { # 70d # 17d }
ELSE 57 CF                                  ("I'm black")
    [[ 0 2 0 2 0 2 0 2 ]         (Black's startup LAYOUT)
    [ 2 0 2 0 2 0 2 0 ]
    [ 0 2 0 2 0 2 0 2 ]
    [ 0 0 0 0 0 0 0 0 ]
    [ 0 0 0 0 0 0 0 0 ]
    [ 1 0 1 0 1 0 1 0 ]
    [ 0 1 0 1 0 1 0 1 ]
    [ 1 0 1 0 1 0 1 0 ]]
    { # 70d # 27d }
END
PICT SWAP 134 CHR
2 →GROB REPL          (Put a "selection arrow" beside user's color)
'LAYOUT' STO
»
```

Checksum: # 42104d
Bytes: 1927.5

	Stack Arguments	Stack Results
1:	(none)	a real number

Notes: **STARTUP** draws the checkerboard in PICT, prompts the user to choose a color, communicates this choice to the opponent's 48, and sets up pieces on the board to start the game.

If the user chooses a color from the keyboard, then a single-character string identifying the opposite color (**"R"** or **"B"**) is transmitted to the opponent's 48. If the user doesn't choose a color before a **"R"** or **"B"** is received from the other machine, then the 48 acts on that string.

If the user is red, the 48 sets user flag 57 (the "I'm red" flag), initializes **LAYOUT** with red pieces in the first three rows, and calls **REDRAW** to put the pieces from **LAYOUT** in the right places on the board. Similarly, if the user is black, the 48 clears user flag 57, initializes **LAYOUT** with black pieces in the first three rows, and calls **REDRAW**.

REDRAW

```
« PICT { # 0d # 0d } BOARD REPL    (Redraw a blank board)
  1 8
  FOR y
    1 8
    FOR x
      IF x y + 2 MOD              (Only check black squares)
      THEN PICT x y R→C           (Calculate square location)
        'LAYOUT' OVER C→L GET      (Check array contents)
        CASE
          DUP 1 SAME                        (1 is a red piece)
            THEN DROP RPIECE GXOR
            END
          DUP 2 SAME                        (2 is a black piece)
            THEN DROP BPIECE GXOR
            END
          DUP 3 SAME                        (3 is a red king)
            THEN DROP RKING GXOR
            END
          4 SAME                            (4 is a black king)
            THEN BKING GXOR
            END
          DROP2
        END                                          (CASE)
      END                                             (IF)
    NEXT                                      (FOR x loop)
  NEXT                                        (FOR y loop)
»
```

Checksum: # 25345d   Bytes: 296.5

Stack Arguments: (none)   Stack Results: (none)

Notes: REDRAW redraws the pieces on the checkerboard, according to
the contents of LAYOUT. It assumes that BOARD already exists
and redraws part of PICT.

MYMOVE

```
« WHILE 59 FS?                    (Loop to find and complete valid move)
    REPEAT SELECT 0 WAIT VALID      (Select, validate movement)
      CASE
        DUP "X" SAME                  (Invalid move—try again)
          THEN DROP
          END
        DUP "D" SAME                          (End of move)
          THEN DROP 59 CF
          END
        DUP "M" SAME OVER "J" SAME OR     (Move or jump)
          THEN 3 DUPN 3 →LIST →STR
            XMIT DROP              (Tell the other machine...
            MOVEIT 59 CF  ...update LAYOUT, display, end move)
            IF DUP IM 8 ==     (If a piece reaches row 8...
            THEN "K" DUP2 2 →LIST →STR    ..."king me")
              XMIT DROP            (Tell the other machine...
              MOVEIT 59 CF  ...update LAYOUT and display)
            ELSE DROP
            END                                    (IF)
          END
      END                                         (CASE)
    END                          (WHILE ... REPEAT loop)
    IF 59 FC?                              (End of turn?)
    THEN { "D" } →STR XMIT DROP     (Pass token to other 48)
    END
»
```

Checksum: # 43550d
Bytes: 323.5

	Stack Arguments	Stack Results
1:	(none)	(none)

Notes: MYMOVE prompts user to select the piece to move, validates the move, communicates it to the opponent's 48 (sends "M", "J", "K", or "D"), updates LAYOUT and the display, and passes the turn to the opponent (clears flag 59). Notice that if MYMOVE gets an "X" from VALID, it repeats SELECT and VALID until you make a valid move.

THMOVE

```
« OPENIO                          (Necessary to receive data)
   DO
      IF BUFLEN DROP DUP          (Check buffer for input)
      THEN SRECV DROP OBJ→ EVAL   (Read buffer, evaluate list)
         → move                   (Store only Level 1 as local variable)
         « CASE
               move "D" SAME      (Other 48 passes token to me...
                  THEN 59 SF         ...therefore, it's my turn)
                  END
               move "K" SAME                      ("King me")
                  THEN (9,9) SWAP -    (Rotate coordinates)
                   move MOVEIT     (Update LAYOUT and display)
                  END
               move "M" SAME
               move "J" SAME OR                (move or jump)
                  THEN (9,9) ROT -
                     (9,9) ROT -          (Rotate coordinates)
                      move MOVEIT DROP(Update LAYOUT, display)
                  END
            END                                         (CASE)
         »
      ELSE DROP                    (No input in buffer yet)
      END                                      (IF BUFLEN...)
   UNTIL 59 FS?                    (that is, UNTIL my turn)
   END                                     (DO ... UNTIL)
   CLOSEIO                         (To conserve battery power)
»
```

Checksum: # 35460d
Bytes: 322.5

	Stack Arguments	Stack Results
1:	(none)	(none)

THMOVE receives the data string from the opponent's 48, translates it and updates **LAYOUT** and the display accordingly (and sets flag 59). It does not validate the opponent's moves.

SELECT

```
« IF 57 FS?                                          (If I'm red...
   THEN 1 3                                 ...then search for red pieces...
   ELSE 2 4                          ...otherwise, search for black pieces)
   END
   → p1 p2                                     (The search for the pieces)
   « 'LAYOUT' 1                                    (Initialize the search)
     DO GETI                                                  (Search...
     UNTIL DUP p1 == SWAP
        p2 == OR                               ...until a piece is found)
     END
     1 -                                   (Index is 1 count too high)
   »
   SWAP DROP DUP 8 / CEIL SWAP 8 MOD      (Convert counter...
   IF DUP 0 ==
   THEN DROP 8
   END
   SWAP R→C                     ... into a square location—a complex #)
   DO HILITE 0 WAIT                (Highlight the square and wait for...
   UNTIL
     → loc key                                            ...key input)
     « loc HILITE
       CASE
          'key==83.1'                       (Key 2—down 2 squares)
             THEN C→R 2 - OVER 2 MOD 1 + MAX R→C 0
             END
          'key==63.1'                         (Key 8—up 2 squares)
             THEN C→R 2 + OVER 2 MOD 7 + MIN R→C 0
             END
          'key==72.1'                       (Key 4—left 2 squares)
             THEN C→R SWAP 2 - OVER 2 MOD
             1 + MAX SWAP R→C 0
             END
          'key==74.1'                      (Key 6—right 2 squares)
             THEN C→R SWAP 2 + OVER 2 MOD
             7 + MIN SWAP R→C 0
             END
```

```
        'key==64.1 AND RE(loc)<8
        AND IM(loc)<8'                  (Key 9—up and right)
          THEN (1,1) + 0
          END
        'key==62.1 AND RE(loc)>1
        AND IM(loc)<8'                  (Key 7—up and left)
          THEN (-1,1) + 0
          END
        'key==82.1 AND RE(loc)>1
        AND IM(loc)>1'                  (Key 1—down and left)
          THEN (1,1) - 0
          END
        'key==84.1 AND RE(loc)<8
        AND IM(loc)>1'                  (Key 3—down and right)
          THEN (1,-1) + 0
          END
        'key==51.1'      (ENTER key—select highlighted square)
          THEN DUP C→L 'LAYOUT' SWAP GET
            DUP DUP 1 == SWAP 3 == OR      (If the piece
            57 FC? XOR AND      on the square is my color...
          END                      ...return its location to Stack)
          0                                  (Otherwise,...
        END
    »
  END                                        (Repeat the search)
»
```

Checksum: # 43360d
Bytes: 984

	Stack Arguments	Stack Results
1:	(none)	*location of selected piece* (complex)

Notes: SELECT searches LAYOUT for the first occurrence of the user's piece and suggests it as the piece to move. By redefining the numeric keypad as a direction control pad, it also allows the user to move the selector around the board to choose a piece to move. Then, with the highlight on a valid piece, (ENTER) selects the piece. SELECT uses HILITE to draw an inverted box around the indicated square.

Note that to make them applicable to either color, many routines use the XOR command, as in this sequence from SELECT:

```
«  ... DUP 1 == SWAP 3 == OR
   57 FC? XOR AND ...
»
```

This says: "If the square has a red piece and I'm red, OR if the square has a black piece and I'm black ... ", thus eliminating the need for: « ...

```
IF 57 FS?
THEN DUP 1 == SWAP 3 == OR
ELSE DUP 2 == SWAP 4 == OR
END ...
»
```

HILITE

```
« PICT OVER
  GROB 8 8 FF181818181818FF
  GXOR
»
```

<u>Checksum</u>: # 4202d
<u>Bytes</u>: 46

	Stack Arguments	Stack Results
1:	*square location* (complex)	*same square location* (complex)

<u>Notes</u>:   HILITE highlights the indicated square by drawing an inverse box around it. It also "un-highlights" the square.

VALID

```
« OVER DUP
  → oldloc key newloc jumploc
  « CASE
      'key==62.1'                    (Key 7—up and left)
        THEN (-1,1)
        END
      'key==64.1'                    (Key 9—up and right)
        THEN (1,1)
        END
      'key==82.1' oldloc WHOZAT
      2 > AND              (Key 1—down and left—kings only)
        THEN (-1,-1)
        END
      'key==84.1' oldloc WHOZAT
      2 > AND              (Key 3—down and right—kings only)
        THEN (1,-1)
        END
      "X"                            (Invalid key)
    END                                     (CASE)
    IF DUP TYPE 1 ==       (Complex type means a valid key)
    THEN
      → inc                          (Save increment)
      « oldloc inc + DUP C→R    (Calculate new location)
        IF DUP 0 > SWAP 9 < AND SWAP (If in bounds ...
           DUP 0 > SWAP 9 < AND AND
        THEN 'newloc' STO
          IF newloc WHOZAT NOT ... and if nobody's there...
          THEN oldloc newloc "M"    ... then do the move)
          ELSE newloc DUP           (Somebody's there)
            'jumploc' STO
            inc + DUP C→R
            IF DUP 0 > SWAP 9 < AND
              SWAP DUP 0 > SWAP 9 <
              AND AND     (If it's a jump ...and in bounds...
            THEN 'newloc' STO
              IF newloc WHOZAT NOT...far side is vacant
```

```
              jumploc WHOZAT 2 MOD...and ctr. piece
                57 FS? XOR AND       ...is the other guy...
              THEN oldloc newloc "J"      ...then jump)
              ELSE "X"         (Otherwise, not a valid jump)
              END                    (IF far side is vacant)
          ELSE DROP "X"         (Jump is out of bounds)
          END                       (IF jump is in bounds)
        END                             (IF nobody's there)
      ELSE DROP "X"              (Move is out of bounds)
      END                             (IF move is in bounds)
    »
  END                                         (IF valid key)
 »
»
```

Checksum: # 16646d

Bytes: 781

Stack Arguments	Stack Results
3:	*starting location* (complex)
2: *starting location* (complex)	*ending location* (complex)
1: *keycode for move direction*	"J" or "M" or "X"

Notes: VALID validates the proposed move passed to it from MYMOVE. The contents of the string output at Stack Level 1 depend on whether the move is a valid Jump, a valid simple Move, or an invalid proposed move ("X"). In the case of an invalid move proposal, no location values are returned in Levels 2 and 3. VALID doesn't check for "king me" opportunities; MYMOVE does.

VALID uses WHOZAT to determine the target square's current occupant.

MOVEIT

```
« 0
  → move piece
  « IF move "M" SAME
       move "J" SAME OR                        (Move or Jump)
    THEN
       → oldloc newloc          (Store start and end locations)
       « 'LAYOUT' oldloc C→L         (Get piece from LAYOUT)
         DUP2 GET 'piece' STO
         0 PUT                  (Blank out old LAYOUT location)
         'LAYOUT' newloc C→L
         piece PUT            (Put piece in new LAYOUT location)
         CASE                     (Select the appropriate grob)
            'piece==1'
               THEN RPIECE
               END
            'piece==2'
               THEN BPIECE
               END
            'piece==3'
               THEN RKING
               END
            'piece==4'
               THEN BKING
               END
         END                                       (CASE)
         'piece' STO          (Store the grob in place of the #)
         PICT oldloc piece GXOR    (Blank out old location)
         PICT newloc piece GXOR  (Put piece in new location)
         IF move "J" SAME      (Extra work needed for jumps...
         THEN oldloc newloc + 2 /    ...find jumped square
            'LAYOUT' OVER C→L 0 PUT    ...blank its LAYOUT
            PICT SWAP # 8d # 8d          location and its
            BLANK NEG REPL              board location)
         END
         newloc    (Dummy Stack value—killed by ... END)
       »
    END                              (IF Move or jump)
```

```
IF move "K" SAME                        ("King me")
THEN
    → loc                               (Store location)
    « 'LAYOUT' loc C→L          (Get piece from LAYOUT...
      DUP2 GET DUP
      'piece' STO 2 + PUT   ...and replace it with a king)
      PICT loc # 8d # 8d
      BLANK NEG REPL           (Blank out board location...
      PICT loc
      CASE
          'piece==1'    ... and replace it with a red king...
              THEN RKING
              END
          'piece==2'                 ...or a black king)
              THEN BKING
              END
      END                                    (CASE)
      GXOR                      (The actual replacement)
    »
    END                                (IF "king me")
  »
»
```

Checksum: # 56746d
Bytes: 780.5

	Stack Arguments	Stack Results
3:	*starting location* (complex)	
2:	*ending location* (complex)	
1:	"J" or "M" or "K"	(none)

Notes: MOVEIT updates LAYOUT and PICT according to the move data
received from other processes. For a "K" ("king me"), the piece's
location is the Level-2 argument, with no Level-3 argument.

WHOZAT

```
« 'LAYOUT' SWAP C→L GET
»
```

Checksum: # 5341d
Bytes: 46.5

Stack Arguments	Stack Results
1: *square location* (complex)	value of LAYOUT there (0-4)

Notes: WHOZAT determines "who's at" a given location on the board.

C→L

```
« C→R SWAP 2 →LIST
»
```

Checksum: # 34716d
Bytes: 27.5

Stack Arguments	Stack Results
1: *square location* (complex)	array index { # *row* # *col* }

Notes: C→L converts a complex number to an array index.

MKBOARD

```
« PICT PURGE                              (Start with a clean slate)
  (0,-7) PMIN (131,56) PMAX               (Set user limits)
  { # 0d # 0d } PVIEW          (Just for fun, show it being built)
  (0,0) (56,56) BOX                       (Outline of the board)
  7 56
  FOR y
     0 49
     FOR x
        IF x y + 2 MOD NOT    (Sum of row and column of black
        THEN PICT x y R→C       square is not odd in this case)
        GROB 8 8 FFFFFFFFFFFFFFFF GOR    (Fill black square)
        END
        7
     STEP
     7
  STEP
  PICT (0,0) (56,56) SUB
  'BOARD' STO                             (Store as BOARD)
»
```

Checksum: # 65383d   Bytes: 315.5

Stack Arguments: (none)   Stack Results: (none)

Notes: MKBOARD makes a blank checkerboard and stores the grob under the variable name BOARD.

A Calendar Demo

With its time and date functions, the 48 is certainly equipped to be a time management tool. One of the features in most electronic time managers is some kind of perpetual calendar, usually presented in the classic seven-column format. As a final little demo, here's an example of what you could do.

Description

The program CALEND displays the current month in seven-column format, offering unshifted menu keys to increment the day, month and year; and ⟵-shifted menu keys to decrement the day, month and year. Press the **EXIT** key to exit the program.

CALEND uses DISP to build the calendar, then turns it into a grob via LCD→. The grob's contents are stored in PICT, and the graphics display is frozen—with the custom menu line displayed—via PVIEW -1 WAIT.

Note that CALEND doesn't use PICT STO to store the calendar in PICT. When the HP 48 executes PICT STO, it resizes PICT to zero, then to the size of the new grob. If your graphics display is active during this time (for example, during a PVIEW), you will see "snow" fill your screen momentarily. This is a graphical representation of part of the HP 48's memory and is displayed while the machine is resizing PICT.

However, since the REPL command does not cause PICT to be resized. CALEND uses PICT { #0d #0d } ROT REPL, instead of PICT STO, thus avoiding the "snow."

The **DAY** and ⬅ **DAY** menu keys in CALEND are not active, although "hooks" (entry points) are included in here so that you can use them to increment/decrement the days as you wish.

Of course, CALEND could also be embellished to do other useful things: set and clear appointments, create "to-do" lists, and do other time-management tasks.

Subroutines

MYR: is the major subroutine behind CALEND. Note that its algorithm uses DISP and not PVIEW to do the display. MYR was written and modified by several members of the CHIP HP48 user's group. The version presented here was developed by Ron Johnson and is used with his permission—and with much appreciation.

CALEND

```
« RCLMENU
  DATE DUP IP SWAP FP 100 * DUP IP SWAP FP 1E4 *
  → menu m d y
  « IFERR
    DO
        m y MYR                         (Create the calendar)
        LCD→ PICT { #0d #0d } ROT REPL  (Avoid snow)
        { { "DAY" } { "MON" } { "YR" } { } { }
          { "EXIT" } }
        TMENU { #0d #0d } PVIEW -1 WAIT (Disp. menu)
        → key                           (Wait for keystroke)
        « CASE
            'key==11.1'
              THEN "Not used" DROP      (Increment day)
              END
            'key==11.2'
              THEN "Not used" DROP      (Decrement day)
              END
            'key==12.1'
              THEN                      (Increment month)
                IF 'm==12'
                THEN 1 'm' STO 'y' 1 STO+
                ELSE 'm' 1 STO+
                END
              END
            'key==12.2'
              THEN                      (Decrement month)
                IF 'm==1'
                THEN 12 'm' STO 'y' 1 STO-
                ELSE 'm' 1 STO-
                END
              END
            'key==13.1'
              THEN 'y' 1 STO+           (Increment year)
              END
```

```
          'key==13.2'
            THEN 'y' 1 STO-          (Decrement year)
            END
          'key==16.1'
            THEN 0 DOERR             (Create exit condition)
            END
          1760 .1 BEEP       (Otherwise, beep—invalid key)
     END                                          (CASE)
       »
   UNTIL 0
   END
THEN menu MENU
END
  »
»
```

Checksum: # 29788d
Bytes: 828

	Stack Arguments	Stack Results
1:	(none)	(none)

Notes: CALEND displays a perpetual calendar in classic seven-column
        format. It uses the current system date to determine the first
        month displayed.

```
                  Aug 1990
           S  M  T  W  T  F  S
                     1  2  3  4
           5  6  7  8  9 10 11
          12 13 14 15 16 17 18
          19 20 21 22 23 24 25
          26 27 28 29 30 31
          DAY  MON  YR          EXIT
```

MYR

```
«
  «                                                (Local function g)
     " 1   2   3   4   5   6   7   8   9 10 11 "   (Build a
     "12 13 14 15 16 17 18 19 20 21 22 "    week string)
     "23 24 25 26 27 28 29 30 31" + +
     ROT 3 * 2 - ROT 3 * 1 - SUB
  »
  «                                                (Local function p)
     IF DUP TYPE 7 ==                             (Display the week string)
     THEN INCR OVER SWAP DISP
     END
     DROP
  »
  RCLF 0 0 0 1 0 0
  → m y g p f d n i b e r
  « y 1000000 / m + .01 + DUP 'd' STO
    10.171582 SWAP DDAYS 7 MOD 'i' STO       (Day of week:
                                              0=Sun, 6=Sat)
    IF m 12 ==                          (Figure number of days in month…
    THEN 31                           …where December is a special case)
    ELSE d DUP 1 + DDAYS
    END
    'n' STO CLLCD "        "      (Month-year string—7 spaces)
    "JanFebMarAprMayJunJulAugSepOctNovDec"
    m 3 * DUP 2 - SWAP SUB + " " + STD y + 'r'
    p EVAL
    " S  M  T  W  T  F  S"           (Days-of-week header)
    IF n i + 35 ≤                   (Leave it out if it doesn't fit)
    THEN 'r'
    END
    p EVAL 7 i - 'e' STO i 3 *
    "                 " DUP + 1 ROT SUB   (First row—9 spaces)
    b e g EVAL + 'r' p EVAL            (Display first row)
    DO e 1 + 'b' STO e 7 + n MIN
       'e' STO                        (Build subsequent rows)
       b e g EVAL 'r' p EVAL        (Display subsequent rows)
```

```
    UNTIL e n ==
    END
    3 FREEZE f STOF
  »
»
```

Checksum: # 61525d
Bytes: 844.5

Stack Arguments	Stack Results
2: *month (real number from 1 to 12)*	
1: *year (real number ≥ 1582)*	(none)

Notes: MYR draws the calendar for any given month and year (the earliest allowable month is November, 1582).

More Suggestions

Now that you've seen some working examples of 48 graphics, you may be speculating on the infinite possibilities. Here's a suggestion or two:

- The 48 has enough graphics power that you could come up with a great PAINT program or grob editor for it, with a display similar to the one shown below. At a menu line, the user would select from the available tools—and submenus would select different brush or fill patterns for each respective tool. A vertical menu on the right side could be used, via the arrow keys, for object/variable management or other purposes. Then the rest of the display would be a window into the grob, which could be scanned as needed. The current grob would not reside in PICT, but portions of it would be displayed in PICT when being edited.

  PAINT would use KEY and WAIT to redefine the keyboard as appropriate. And note that several of the routines developed in this book could be incorporated into PAINT, too.

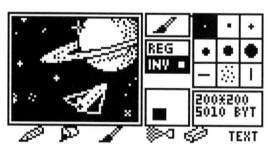

The only drawbacks—as with all graphics routines—are memory use and speed. Consider those your challenges. After all, you're the judge as to what's acceptable and usable.

- Some of the most intriguing home video games are the role-playing adventure games, where the hero negotiates some large playing field, encountering monsters and other baddies.

Such a game on the 48, for example, could use an intricately detailed 800×800 grob as the playing field, and dozens of little 8×8 grobs for the hero and the baddies. It wouldn't be hard.

- You've seen a checkers game. How about other familiar games (Battleship, Tetris, hangman, cards, etc.)? Your only limits are your imagination (and spare time).

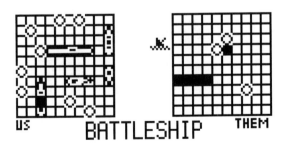

9: GRAPHICS BEYOND THE 48

(OR, "WHAT'S THAT FUNNY HOLE IN THE TOP OF MY CALCULATOR?")

Of course, graphics on the 48 are nice in and of themselves, but their utility increases when you can transfer them to other machines.

Printing Graphics on the Infrared Printer

Although it is possible to send low-level graphics commands to the HP82240A/B infrared printer, it is faster and more efficient to use the built-in commands PR1 and PRVAR.

PR1 prints the grob in Stack Level 1. PRVAR prints the grob whose variable name appears in Level 1. To print more than one grob, you can use a list of variable names as the PRVAR argument. Note that PRVAR prefaces each object with a blank line and the variable name.

The HP 82240A/B printer can print only 166 dot columns. For a grob wider than 166 pixels, the printer will print the graphic in strips, with "cut here" dotted lines separating the strips, so you can paste them together later. You can avoid this problem if you have an Epson-compatible or PCL-compatible printer (keep reading...).

To print the text representation of a grob, (GROB *x* *y* *ddd...*), it's best to convert the grob to a string, a list or a program, and print it via PR1 (or, better yet, upload it to a personal computer and print it from there).

Printing Graphics on a Larger Printer

To print a graphic on a larger printer, you must translate the grob from 48 language into a language that the larger printer can understand. Recall from Chapter 4 that a grob is an object of the format

$$\text{GROB} \quad x \quad y \quad bbbbbb....$$

where x and y are the width and height, respectively, in pixels, and $bbbbbb....$ is a hexadecimal bitmap of the grob—in the 48's "reversed" notation.

Before you can print the grob, you must separate these three pieces of information for the printer. This program takes a grob from Stack Level 1 and separates the information into its three parts on the Stack:

DISSECT

```
« →STR DUP SIZE 6 SWAP SUB
  0 1
  FOR n
    DUP DUP " " POS SWAP OVER
    1 - 1 SWAP SUB OBJ→
    ROT ROT 1 + OVER SIZE SUB
  NEXT
»
```

Checksum: # 48062d   Bytes: 102

	Stack Arguments	Stack Results
3:		x (a real number)
2:		y (a real number)
1:	GROB x y $bbbbbb....$	$bbbbbb....$(a string)

Now, you'll also recall from the discussion in Chapter 4 (see page 90) that each nybble in the bitmap is presented with the bits reversed from the normal convention.

Here's a table that shows the translation between the 48 bitmap and a "right-reading" bitmap:

48 nybble hex value	bit pattern	reversed bit pattern	"right-reading" hex value
0	0000	0000	0
1	0001	1000	8
2	0010	0100	4
3	0011	1100	C
4	0100	0010	2
5	0101	1010	A
6	0110	0110	6
7	0111	1110	E
8	1000	0001	1
9	1001	1001	9
A	1010	0101	5
B	1011	1101	D
C	1100	0011	3
D	1101	1011	B
E	1110	0111	7
F	1111	1111	F

Notice the symmetry in the table: E translates to 7, and 7 translates to E, for example. Also, 0, 6, 9 and F translate into themselves, because their bit patterns are symmetrical.

From the translation table given above, you can assemble a string to represent the translated bitmap. The string is composed of the entries in the "right-reading" column of the table: `"084C2A6E195D3B7F"`. Thus, in a program, translating a nybble becomes as simple as

```
« ... "0123456789ABCDEF"
     "084C2A6E195D3B7F"
     ROT POS DUP SUB ...
  »
```

And you can build this sequence into a routine for translating bitmaps of any size. The following program will take a bitmap string from Stack Level 1 and replace it with a translated string:

TRANSLATE

```
« DUP SIZE
   → map len
   « 1 len
     FOR j
       "0123456789ABCDEF" "084C2A6E195D3B7F"
       map j j SUB POS DUP SUB
       map j ROT REPL 'map' STO
     NEXT
     map
   »
»
```

Checksum: # 58829d   Bytes: 171.5

	Stack Arguments	Stack Results
1:	*bbbbbb*....(a string)	*bbbbbb*....(a string)

Note: To get your original string back again, just execute TRANSLATE a second time—the translation table is symmetrical.

Formatting Output for the Printer

The most common printer protocols in use today are Epson and PCL. Most printers—including laser printers—offer Epson compatibility, either built-in or as an option. PCL is the Printer Control Language used by all HP printers, including the HP LaserJet and DeskJet. Most laser printers offer built-in PCL compatibility.

The main difference between the two protocols is that PCL uses _raster_ graphics—receiving data in 8-dot _rows_—while Epson uses _column_ graphics—receiving data in 8-dot _columns_:

PCL-Protocol Printers   Epson-Protocol Printers

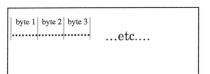 

Each byte here represents 8 dots* of graphic output.

In PCL, each bit represents one dot in a _row_, with the least significant bit on the right. Bytes are sent to the printer as characters, so a _row_ of four black dots followed by four white dots would have a character value of # 11110000b (that's # F0h or # 240d).

By contrast, in Epson, the least significant bit goes at the bottom of a _column_ of bits. Bytes are sent to the printer as characters, so a _column_ of four black dots atop four white dots would have a character value of # 11110000b (that's # F0h or # 240d).

*Dots are _printer_ data, as opposed to pixels, which are _display_ data.

So suppose you wanted to print this 19×15 graphics object:

On the 48, you would describe this object as

```
GROB 19 15
18F040  160340  110440  900840  900840
540150  5A8250  540150  500050  540150
98F840  900840  110440  160340  18F040
```

(rows are separated for clarity)

Running the bitmap string through TRANSLATE would then give you:

```
81F020  860C20  880220  900120  900120
A208A0  A514A0  A208A0  A000A0  A208A0
91F120  900120  880220  860C20  81F020
```

To successfully print the grob, a PCL printer would need to see a string of the form "x̄ồ ▶■...", where

    x̄ is CHR(129) or 81h
    ồ is CHR(240) or F0h
      is CHR(32) or 20h (<space>)
 ▶ is CHR(134) or 86h
 ■ is CHR(12) or 0Ch (<Form Feed>)

As you can see, the PCL data string can be readily obtained directly from the **TRANSLATE**'d bitmap string (compare for yourself).

On the other hand, an Epson printer would expect to see a string of the form "Ÿ■ ■ ■ ..." where

  Ÿ is CHR(255) or FFh
 ■ is CHR(0)   or 00h (<NUL>)
 ■ is CHR(7)   or 07h (<BEL>)
 ■ is CHR(24)   or 18h (<CAN>)
    is CHR(32)   or 20h (<space>)

This Epson string is not so easy to obtain from the **TRANSLATE**'d string. In fact, it's probably easier to write an Epson print program on the 48 which stores the grob in PICT and builds the Epson data string by testing individual pixels.

Printer Control Codes

When printing graphics, you must send control codes to the printer, warning it that the next batch of data it receives is graphics data instead of text. Otherwise, your printer will act unpredictably.

For PCL printers, use these commands, each sent as a string:*

"<ESC>*rA"   *(Start raster graphics)*

"<ESC>*bnW..."   *(Print the next "n" bytes as graphics data. For your*
                     19×15 grob, you'd repeat this string 15 times—once
                     for each row. The first part of the command, then,
                     would be "<ESC>*b3Wx̆8̆ <ESC>*b3W▶■ ..."

"<CR><LF>"   *(Print the buffer, advance to the next line and*
                     return to the left margin)

"<ESC>*rB"   *(End raster graphics)*

These PCL control codes are for the HP ThinkJet, QuietJet, DeskJet and LaserJet printers, and any other printers which understand PCL.

Keep in mind that your display grobs printed at 300 dpi will become postage-stamp size. But on some printers, (for example, the DeskJet and LaserJet), you can select from different dot pitches. To change dot pitches in PCL printers, use these commands.

"<ESC>*t75R"   *Set dot pitch to 75 dpi—DeskJet or LaserJet only)*
"<ESC>*t100R"   *Set dot pitch to 100 dpi—DeskJet or LaserJet only)*
"<ESC>*t150R"   *Set dot pitch to 150 dpi—DeskJet or LaserJet only)*
"<ESC>*t300R"   *Set dot pitch to 300 dpi—DeskJet or LaserJet only)*
"<ESC>*t96R"   *Set dot pitch to 96 dpi—QuietJet only—default)*
"<ESC>*t192R"   *Set dot pitch to 192 dpi—QuietJet only)*

---

*<ESC> is CHR(27) ("Escape"); <CR> is CHR(13) ("Carriage Return"); <LF> is CHR(10) ("Line Feed").

For Epson printers, use these commands, each sent as a string:*

"<ESC>A8"	*(Set the line spacing to 8-dot rows)*
"<ESC>K̇nm..."	*(Print the next "n+(256×m)" bytes as graphics data. For the 48, usually you'll have less than 256 bytes per row, so m=0. In the example grob, you have 19 columns of data, so n will be CHR(19); you have 15 rows of data, so you'll have to send such a string twice:* **"<ESC>K̇ ■ ■ ÿ ■ ■ ■ ..."** and **"<ESC>K̇ ■ ■ ..."** *The first two ■ ■ in each string are CHR(19) and CHR(0), respectively, and then the actual data commences—with ÿ ■ ■ ■ ... , for example, in the first string, as shown on page 245)*
"<CR><LF>"	*(Print the buffer, advance to the next line and return to the left margin)*
"<ESC>2"	*(Reset the line spacing to 6 lines per inch)*

These Epson control codes are for printers that print at 96 dpi in "single-density" mode (<ESC>K̇ selects "single-density" printing). The codes will work with printers of other dot pitches, also—even with the 300-dpi Epson emulation on most laser printers. But as you know, at that resolution, your 131×64 display-sized grobs start looking like postage stamps. You'll need to modify your printing program to print a square of several dots for each pixel in your grob.

For more information on printer control codes, consult the owner's manual for your printer.

---

*<ESC> is CHR(27) ("Escape"); <CR> is CHR(13) ("Carriage Return"); <LF> is CHR(10) ("Line Feed").

The basic algorithm for a printer driver is as follows:

1. Clear system flag −33, to route non-printing I/O through the infrared port, and set system flag −34, to route printer output through the serial port.

2. **Epson:** Set the line spacing on your printer—typically 8 for most Epson printers. **PCL:** Set the dot pitch, if applicable; enable raster graphics.

3. **PCL:** Use the "translation string" to translate the grob data to a "right-reading" bitmap. **Epson:** Store the grob in PICT and extract data, 1 column of 8 pixels at a time.

4. Build the graphics data string for the first row of data. Preface it with the appropriate printer control code (see previous page).

5. Build data strings for all subsequent rows of data. Preface each string with the appropriate printer control code, and append them to the data string (for every case with the 48, the printer control codes will be identical).

6. Send the data string to the printer, making sure to end the line with a <CR> only. Note that on the 48, the <CR><LF> is automatic. But you can disable the <LF> by setting system flag −38, executing 0 TRANSIO, and then storing a null string ("") in the fourth field of PRTPAR.

7. **Epson:** Reset the line spacing to 6 lines per inch. **PCL:** End or disable raster graphics; reset the dot pitch, if necessary.

8. Restore system flags, if necessary.

Avoiding Problems

Laser printers don't print to the paper until they receive a <Form Feed>, which is CHR(12). If you're printing to a laser printer, you won't see any output until either the end of the page has been reached, or you send a CHR(12) to the printer.

However, if you store this program, FF, in your **HOME** directory, then you can send a <Form Feed> simply by executing FF, or by including it in any program:

> FF: « 12 CHR PR1 DROP
>   »
> Checksum: # 22456d   Bytes: 34.5

It is strongly recommended that you use handshaking on both your printer and the 48. This gives the printer a chance to say "wait a minute, I'm busy" without either the 48 or the printer losing any data. You can select XON/XOFF handshaking on the 48 by setting the fourth parameter in the IOPAR reserved variable to 1 (for more information on using IOPAR, see Chapter 32 of the Owner's Manual).

Two Sample Printing Programs

Combining all the above information into one place, you should be able
to create a program to suit your needs and your printer. Use these two
programs as examples.

PRGROB1

```
« DUP SIZE PICT RCLF                    (Save defaults)
   STD                          (Select standard numeric notation)
   27 CHR "A8" +                         (Set dot pitch to 8)
   27 CHR "K" +                       (Beginning of data string)
   27 CHR "2" +                     (Reset dot pitch to default)
   0                           (Temporary storage variable)
   → gr x y pictx flags dp8 dat re t
   « gr PICT STO
     -33 CF -34 SF -38 SF   (IR I/O, serial printing, auto LF)
     dp8 PR1 DROP
     x B→R 256 MOD CHR dat
     OVER + 'dat' STO        (Build <ESC>K to <ESC>Kn)
     x B→R SWAP NUM - 256 / CHR
     dat SWAP + 'dat' STO    (Build <ESC>Kn to <ESC>Knm)
     ""                        (Initialize data string)
     0 y B→R 8 / CEIL
     FOR bigrow
        dat +                         (Initialize line data)
        0 x B→R
        FOR col
           0 't' STO                (Initialize column data)
           0 7
           FOR row                       (Test each pixel)
              col R→B
              bigrow 8 * row + R→B
              2 →LIST PIX?            (Returns 1 or 0)
              2 7 row - ^ * 't' STO+ (Increment col. data)
           NEXT                            (Next row)
```

```
          t CHR +
       NEXT                              (Next column)
     NEXT                                (Next big row)
     PR1 DROP re PR1 DROP         (Print grob, reset printer)
     pictx PICT STO flags STOF      (Restore previous states)
   »
»
```

Checksum: # 61444d
Bytes: 549

	Stack Arguments	Stack Results
1:	GROB *x* *y* *bbbbbb....*	(none)

Notes: PRGROB1 prints a grob on an Epson-compatible printer, de-
stroying PICT in the process.

```
« DISSECT TRANSLATE                (Get width, height and bitmap)
  RCLF                             (Save previous states)
  STD                              (Select standard numeric notation)
  27 CHR "*t75R" +      (Set dot pitch to 75 dpi—96 for QuietJet)
  27 CHR "*rA" +                   (Begin raster graphics)
  27 CHR "*rB" +                   (End raster graphics)
  27 CHR "*b" +                    (Beginning of data string)
  0                                (Temporary storage variable)
  → x y map flags dp75 begrg endrg dat t
  « -33 CF -34 SF -38 SF                    (IR I/O,...
    0 TRANSIO 'PRTPAR' DUP
    3 1000 PUT 4 "" PUT        ...serial printing, disable LF)
    endrg PR1 DROP          (Garbage collection on the printer)
    dp75 PR1 DROP                        (Set dot pitch)
    begrg PR1 DROP                   (Begin raster graphics)
    map SIZE y /
    DUP 't' STO                  (Data string length per row)
    dat SWAP 2 / + "W"
    + 'dat' STO                (Build <ESC>b to <ESC>bnW)
    ""                              (Initialize data string)
    1 y
    FOR row
       dat +                        (Initialize line data)
       row 1 - t * 1 + row t *
       FOR char
          map char
          DUP 1 + SUB           (Read bitmap for next 8 bits)
          "#" SWAP + "h" + OBJ→
          B→R CHR +                (Add to data string)
          2
       STEP                             (Next character)
    NEXT                                    (Next row)
    PR1 DROP endrg PR1 DROP (Prt. grob, end raster graphics)
    12 CHR PR1 DROP                 (Form feed—optional)
    flags STOF                    (Restore previous states)
  »
»
```

<u>Checksum</u>: # 23770d
<u>Bytes</u>: 595

	<u>Stack Arguments</u>	<u>Stack Results</u>
1:	GROB *x* *y* *bbbbbb*....	(none)

<u>Notes</u>: PRGROB2 prints a grob on a PCL-compatible printer.

The Hard Work's Already Done

Fortunately, HP has already provided print routines that do all this for you, in the form of two public-domain libraries called EPSPRINT.LIB and PCLPRINT.LIB.

These libraries are available on the HP 82208A Serial Interface Kit disk, or are downloadable from the HP Calculator Bulletin Board System (BBS). Instructions for using the libraries are located in two other files called EPSPRINT.TXT and PCLPRINT.TXT.*

Using EPSPRINT

Once installed, the EPSPRINT library appears in the Library menu as **EPPRT**. When selected, it shows this menu: **EPOFF** **EPON** **MAG**

Pressing **EPON** modifies PRTPAR and system flags –33 and –34 to send all printer output to an Epson-compatible printer over the serial interface, using XON/XOFF flow control. It uses a "hook" in the 48's operating system to activate the Epson graphics printer driver. Text is output in the printer's current font, and graphics is output at 60 dpi (you can modify PRTPAR to set it to 120 or 240 dpi, but 240 dpi is not recommended).

Pressing **EPOFF** returns PRTPAR and flags –33 and –34 to their turn-on states, allowing you to continue using the infrared printer. You may ignore **EPOFF** if you don't use an infrared printer.

*For more information on the HP BBS, contact HP Calculator Technical Support at (503) 757-2004.

Pressing **MAG** with an argument of $1, 2$ or 4 causes EPPRT to use the given magnification factor in printing graphics (the default is 2). For example, 4 **MAG** causes every pixel in the grob to be printed as a square, 4 dots × 4 dots.

All 48 printing commands *except ON-PRINT* work normally with EPPRT. ON-PRINT does unpredictable nasties with your printer and should not be used. Use PRLCD instead. Also, you can automate your Epson printing somewhat by storing these routines in your **HOME** directory:

EPR1:   « EPON PR1 EPOFF
            »
            <u>Checksum</u>: # 18483d   <u>Bytes</u>: 37

EPRVAR: « EPON PRVAR EPOFF
            »
            <u>Checksum</u>: # 51587d   <u>Bytes</u>: 39

Using *PCLPRINT*

The PCLPRINT library appears in the Library menu as `HPPRT`. When you select it, you see this menu: `HPOFF` `HPON` `DPI` `MAG`

Similar to `EPON` in EPPRT, `HPON` also modifies PRTPAR and system flags –33 and –34, but it does so in order to send all printer output to a PCL-compatible printer over the serial interface, using XON/XOFF flow control. It, too, uses a "hook" in the HP-48's operating system to activate the PCL graphics printer driver. Text is output in the printer's current font.

`HPOFF` acts much like `EPOFF`, allowing you to continue using the infrared printer (and likewise, you may ignore `HPOFF` if you aren't using an infrared printer).

`DPI` takes an argument from Stack Level 1 and uses it to set the printer to the proper dot pitch. This could be 75, 150 or 300 dpi for a DeskJet or LaserJet (doesn't apply to other printers).

Unlike the `MAG` in EPPRT, the `MAG` in HPPRT can take any integer as an argument for the magnification factor. Entering n `MAG` causes every pixel in the grob to be printed as a square, n dots × n dots (no default is given, but it appears to be 1).

For a 300 dpi printer, 1 `MAG` will give you a postage-stamp sized image of a 131×64 grob. A grob printed at 2 `MAG` is about the same scale as an HP82240A/B printout, and a grob printed at 6 `MAG` is about the same scale as the 48's LCD display.

All 48 printing commands *except ON-PRINT* work normally with HPPRT. ON-PRINT has the same problems in HPPRT as in EPPRT.

However, when printing to a LaserJet series printer, note that the LaserJet prints to a *buffer*, not directly to the paper. The buffer is printed onto the paper either when the buffer is full, or when a form-feed character (ASCII # 12d) is sent to the printer. So if you're putting several graphics on one page, be sure to send a CR (there's a ▌CR▐ key in the PRINT menu) after each grob to provide some white space.

When you're ready to eject the page, you'll need to send a <Form Feed> character to the printer (you can use your FF program to do this).

Also, you can automate your PCL printing somewhat by storing the following two routines in your HOME directory.

HPR1:   « HPON PR1 HPOFF FF
             »
             Checksum: # 38722d   Bytes: 42.5

HPRVAR: « HPON PRVAR HPOFF FF
             »
             Checksum: # 33078d   Bytes: 44.5

You may omit the FF's in these two routines if you're not using a LaserJet, or if you wish to put multiple printouts on one page.

Printing Graphics on a Pen Plotter

With the advent of high-resolution, wide-carriage, color dot-matrix printers, pen plotters seem to be disappearing quickly. Still, a pen plotter can be used as a graphics output device. The algorithm for a plotter driver is very simple—and fast, since pixels can be printed "on the fly," without waiting to build large graphics command strings.

The basic algorithm for a plotter driver is as follows:

1. Set the pen width and pixel spacing for the plotter—typically 0.3 mm or 0.65 mm.

2. *Either* use TRANSLATE to translate the grob's data to a "right-reading" bitmap, and then process the bitmap; *or* store the grob in PICT, and scan PICT, pixel by pixel.

3. With pen UP, scan the paper, row by row. At each pixel location, put the pen DOWN if the pixel is "dark" in that location, and draw a small square. Then put the pen UP again to resume scanning.

You may also wish to draw an outline box around your grob after it is completed.

Grobs and Other Computers

Since integrated text and graphics are taken for granted on computers these days, it would be nice to be able to include grobs in your computer work.

For example, if you're writing a lab report on your PC and have some important data stored in your 48, you can upload the numeric data to your computer, but you might also want to include the impressive graph you made on the 48 to avoid having to duplicate it in a spreadsheet.

Or suppose your report contains several long, involved equations like the ones in Chapter 3 in this book. Using the two-dimensional EW version is an easy way to get "textbook" notation in your report without having to buy the mathematics add-on for your word processor.

By virtue of their (admittedly) superior raw computing power, conversion of raw grobs to computer-format graphics is best done by the computers. DISSECT and TRANSLATE are trivial on a PC, but the grob-to-graphics conversion problem is complicated by the fact that there doesn't yet exist a standard computer graphics format.

Here, Hewlett-Packard comes to the rescue again. HP has developed programs called GROB2TIF.EXE and TIF2GROB.EXE for MS-DOS computers, and one called GROBer for Macintosh computers.

GROB2TIF.EXE converts grobs to TIFF files, which can be used, or at least converted into something else, by the most popular word-processing and desktop-publishing programs. TIF2GROB.EXE converts TIFF files to grobs for use on the 48.

The GROBer allows you to convert grobs to Macintosh graphics for use with any Macintosh package, and to convert Macintosh graphics to grobs. Some of the finest 48 graphics to appear to date were taken from the Macintosh.

GROB2TIF.EXE is available on the HP82208A Serial Interface Kit disk for MS-DOS machines. The GROBer is available on the HP82209 Serial Interface Kit disk for Macintoshes. Both programs are also available from the HP Calculator BBS (see the footnote on page 254).

TIF2GROB.EXE is available only from the HP Calculator BBS.

Graphics Between Two 48's

It's hard to think of a serious use for two-machine graphics besides games or cool-looking demos, but some people take their games and their demos very seriously.

As you've seen with the CHKRS program, it is quite straightforward to create some two-player games on the 48, with two machines connected via IR or the serial port.

A well-behaved game program shows the board from the player's point of view and passes a token to keep track of whose move it was. A *skilled* game program checks for invalid moves (such as moving backwards in checkers) and allow for complex moves (such as double-jumping in checkers), and—of course—it would keep score.

Final Thoughts

This book is only the beginning. It has shown you just a few of the great graphics tricks the 48 can do, and how you can use these graphics tricks to your advantage. And in the process, hopefully, you've become more comfortable with the machine, by working through the exercises and trying the applications (and maybe you also have a better idea of how to use the EquationWriter, the Solver and the Plotter).

All that remains is for you to find real uses for these tools—applications in your job, studies or hobbies. As you use the 48, you will undoubtedly become more skilled with it and thus it will become the more useful to you in return. Again, remember what your high school band teacher told you:

"Proficiency comes through practice."

Above all, have fun!

More Graphite Grobs

Famous Oatmeal Cookies *

¾ Cup vegetable shortening
1 Cup firmly packed brown sugar
½ Cup granulated sugar
1 egg
¼ Cup water
1 teaspoon vanilla
3 Cups rolled oats, uncooked
1 Cup all-purpose flour
1 teaspoon salt (optional)
½ teaspoon baking soda

Preheat oven to 350°F. Beat together shortening, sugars, egg, water and vanilla until creamy. Add combined remaining ingredients; mix well.

(Finally, Valerie says to fold in 1 Cup of semi-sweet chocolate chips.)

Drop by rounded teaspoonfuls onto greased cookie sheet. Bake at 350°F for 12 to 15 minutes.

* Recipe courtesy of the Quaker Oats company.

APPENDICES

A: Review of the Hexadecimal Number System

"Hexadecimal" is a word derived from the Latin roots for *six* ("hexa-") and *ten* ("decimal"). It is a form of expressing numbers in base sixteen. "Hexadecimal" is often abbreviated to "hex."

The Decimal System as an Example of Counting Systems

Most human beings count in the *decimal*, or base-ten, number system (though you may have heard also of the *binary*, or base-two, number system). In base ten, you use the numerals from 0 to 9. To count past nine, you need some way to indicate the overflow, so you use a second digit—the "tens" digit—to count the "number of overflows." Likewise, when you run out of digits to express the "overflows," you add a third digit—a "hundreds" digit—to count the "overflows of overflows." And so on, until you have enough digits to express any given number.

So, proceeding from right to left, the first digit represents the number of "ones," or 10^0, in the number; the second digit represents the number of whole sets of ten (10^1); the third digit represents the number of whole sets of a hundred (10^2), etc. Thus, the nth digit represents the number of whole sets of 10^{n-1} in the number.

So you could think of the number 3401 as:

$$3\times10^3 + 4\times10^2 + 0\times10^1 + 1\times10^0$$

Significant Digits

Obviously, changing the leftmost digit in the number has a greater effect on the number than changing the rightmost digit. That is, the leftmost digit is the *most significant digit*; and the rightmost digit is the *least significant digit*. For example, if you see a house selling for $63,499 and one selling for $63,500, you'd say they both cost the same. One dollar isn't very significant compared to sixty thousand dollars.

The right-to-left order of increasing significance is a convention used in other place-value numbering systems, including binary and hexadecimal.

Hexadecimal Values

Computers count in binary, using only the numerals 0 and 1. That's difficult for humans to comprehend and uses a lot of space in displays and printouts. A more convenient way to organize binary data is to group the binary digits (*bits*) together in groups of four, and assign each group a single value.

Look at the table on the opposite page. You'll see that a group of four bits can range from 0000, with a value of zero, to 1111, with a value of fifteen. That's sixteen values, which is why sixteen—hexadecimal—is such a convenient number base to use when working with computers.

Of course, when expressing number values, you have only ten conventional Arabic numerals (0-9). But when counting in hexadecimal, you must go all the way to fifteen before adding a second numeral as a "counter of overflows." So the *letters* A-F are used as numerals to represent the values ten through fifteen in hexadecimal.

Decimal	Binary	Hex
0	0000	0
1	0001	1
2	0010	2
3	0011	3
4	0100	4
5	0101	5
6	0110	6
7	0111	7
8	1000	8
9	1001	9
10	1010	A
11	1011	B
12	1100	C
13	1101	D
14	1110	E
15	1111	F

In the 48, integer objects can be expressed as binary, decimal, hex or octal (base eight). The # sign before the number means that it's an integer, and the b/d/h/o suffix indicates its number base. You can convert these integer number formats from one base to another using the 48's BASE menu, or use the following table (for the corresponding 48 display characters, see Appendix C in the Owner's Manual):

Binary	Decimal	Hex.		Binary	Decimal	Hex.
# 00000000b	# 000d	# 00h		# 00100000b	# 032d	# 20h
# 00000001b	# 001d	# 01h		# 00100001b	# 033d	# 21h
# 00000010b	# 002d	# 02h		# 00100010b	# 034d	# 22h
# 00000011b	# 003d	# 03h		# 00100011b	# 035d	# 23h
# 00000100b	# 004d	# 04h		# 00100100b	# 036d	# 24h
# 00000101b	# 005d	# 05h		# 00100101b	# 037d	# 25h
# 00000110b	# 006d	# 06h		# 00100110b	# 038d	# 26h
# 00000111b	# 007d	# 07h		# 00100111b	# 039d	# 27h
# 00001000b	# 008d	# 08h		# 00101000b	# 040d	# 28h
# 00001001b	# 009d	# 09h		# 00101001b	# 041d	# 29h
# 00001010b	# 010d	# 0Ah		# 00101010b	# 042d	# 2Ah
# 00001011b	# 011d	# 0Bh		# 00101011b	# 043d	# 2Bh
# 00001100b	# 012d	# 0Ch		# 00101100b	# 044d	# 2Ch
# 00001101b	# 013d	# 0Dh		# 00101101b	# 045d	# 2Dh
# 00001110b	# 014d	# 0Eh		# 00101110b	# 046d	# 2Eh
# 00001111b	# 015d	# 0Fh		# 00101111b	# 047d	# 2Fh
# 00010000b	# 016d	# 10h		# 00110000b	# 048d	# 30h
# 00010001b	# 017d	# 11h		# 00110001b	# 049d	# 31h
# 00010010b	# 018d	# 12h		# 00110010b	# 050d	# 32h
# 00010011b	# 019d	# 13h		# 00110011b	# 051d	# 33h
# 00010100b	# 020d	# 14h		# 00110100b	# 052d	# 34h
# 00010101b	# 021d	# 15h		# 00110101b	# 053d	# 35h
# 00010110b	# 022d	# 16h		# 00110110b	# 054d	# 36h
# 00010111b	# 023d	# 17h		# 00110111b	# 055d	# 37h
# 00011000b	# 024d	# 18h		# 00111000b	# 056d	# 38h
# 00011001b	# 025d	# 19h		# 00111001b	# 057d	# 39h
# 00011010b	# 026d	# 1Ah		# 00111010b	# 058d	# 3Ah
# 00011011b	# 027d	# 1Bh		# 00111011b	# 059d	# 3Bh
# 00011100b	# 028d	# 1Ch		# 00111100b	# 060d	# 3Ch
# 00011101b	# 029d	# 1Dh		# 00111101b	# 061d	# 3Dh
# 00011110b	# 030d	# 1Eh		# 00111110b	# 062d	# 3Eh
# 00011111b	# 031d	# 1Fh		# 00111111b	# 063d	# 3Fh

	Binary		Decimal		Hex.		Binary		Decimal		Hex.
#	01000000b	#	064d	#	40h	#	01100000b	#	096d	#	60h
#	01000001b	#	065d	#	41h	#	01100001b	#	097d	#	61h
#	01000010b	#	066d	#	42h	#	01100010b	#	098d	#	62h
#	01000011b	#	067d	#	43h	#	01100011b	#	099d	#	63h
#	01000100b	#	068d	#	44h	#	01100100b	#	100d	#	64h
#	01000101b	#	069d	#	45h	#	01100101b	#	101d	#	65h
#	01000110b	#	070d	#	46h	#	01100110b	#	102d	#	66h
#	01000111b	#	071d	#	47h	#	01100111b	#	103d	#	67h
#	01001000b	#	072d	#	48h	#	01101000b	#	104d	#	68h
#	01001001b	#	073d	#	49h	#	01101001b	#	105d	#	69h
#	01001010b	#	074d	#	4Ah	#	01101010b	#	106d	#	6Ah
#	01001011b	#	075d	#	4Bh	#	01101011b	#	107d	#	6Bh
#	01001100b	#	076d	#	4Ch	#	01101100b	#	108d	#	6Ch
#	01001101b	#	077d	#	4Dh	#	01101101b	#	109d	#	6Dh
#	01001110b	#	078d	#	4Eh	#	01101110b	#	110d	#	6Eh
#	01001111b	#	079d	#	4Fh	#	01101111b	#	111d	#	6Fh
#	01010000b	#	080d	#	50h	#	01110000b	#	112d	#	70h
#	01010001b	#	081d	#	51h	#	01110001b	#	113d	#	71h
#	01010010b	#	082d	#	52h	#	01110010b	#	114d	#	72h
#	01010011b	#	083d	#	53h	#	01110011b	#	115d	#	73h
#	01010100b	#	084d	#	54h	#	01110100b	#	116d	#	74h
#	01010101b	#	085d	#	55h	#	01110101b	#	117d	#	75h
#	01010110b	#	086d	#	56h	#	01110110b	#	118d	#	76h
#	01010111b	#	087d	#	57h	#	01110111b	#	119d	#	77h
#	01011000b	#	088d	#	58h	#	01111000b	#	120d	#	78h
#	01011001b	#	089d	#	59h	#	01111001b	#	121d	#	79h
#	01011010b	#	090d	#	5Ah	#	01111010b	#	122d	#	7Ah
#	01011011b	#	091d	#	5Bh	#	01111011b	#	123d	#	7Bh
#	01011100b	#	092d	#	5Ch	#	01111100b	#	124d	#	7Ch
#	01011101b	#	093d	#	5Dh	#	01111101b	#	125d	#	7Dh
#	01011110b	#	094d	#	5Eh	#	01111110b	#	126d	#	7Eh
#	01011111b	#	095d	#	5Fh	#	01111111b	#	127d	#	7Fh

Binary	Decimal	Hex.		Binary	Decimal	Hex.
# 10000000b	# 128d	# 80h		# 10100000b	# 160d	# A0h
# 10000001b	# 129d	# 81h		# 10100001b	# 161d	# A1h
# 10000010b	# 130d	# 82h		# 10100010b	# 162d	# A2h
# 10000011b	# 131d	# 83h		# 10100011b	# 163d	# A3h
# 10000100b	# 132d	# 84h		# 10100100b	# 164d	# A4h
# 10000101b	# 133d	# 85h		# 10100101b	# 165d	# A5h
# 10000110b	# 134d	# 86h		# 10100110b	# 166d	# A6h
# 10000111b	# 135d	# 87h		# 10100111b	# 167d	# A7h
# 10001000b	# 136d	# 88h		# 10101000b	# 168d	# A8h
# 10001001b	# 137d	# 89h		# 10101001b	# 169d	# A9h
# 10001010b	# 138d	# 8Ah		# 10101010b	# 170d	# AAh
# 10001011b	# 139d	# 8Bh		# 10101011b	# 171d	# ABh
# 10001100b	# 140d	# 8Ch		# 10101100b	# 172d	# ACh
# 10001101b	# 141d	# 8Dh		# 10101101b	# 173d	# ADh
# 10001110b	# 142d	# 8Eh		# 10101110b	# 174d	# AEh
# 10001111b	# 143d	# 8Fh		# 10101111b	# 175d	# AFh
# 10010000b	# 144d	# 90h		# 10110000b	# 176d	# B0h
# 10010001b	# 145d	# 91h		# 10110001b	# 177d	# B1h
# 10010010b	# 146d	# 92h		# 10110010b	# 178d	# B2h
# 10010011b	# 147d	# 93h		# 10110011b	# 179d	# B3h
# 10010100b	# 148d	# 94h		# 10110100b	# 180d	# B4h
# 10010101b	# 149d	# 95h		# 10110101b	# 181d	# B5h
# 10010110b	# 150d	# 96h		# 10110110b	# 182d	# B6h
# 10010111b	# 151d	# 97h		# 10110111b	# 183d	# B7h
# 10011000b	# 152d	# 98h		# 10111000b	# 184d	# B8h
# 10011001b	# 153d	# 99h		# 10111001b	# 185d	# B9h
# 10011010b	# 154d	# 9Ah		# 10111010b	# 186d	# BAh
# 10011011b	# 155d	# 9Bh		# 10111011b	# 187d	# BBh
# 10011100b	# 156d	# 9Ch		# 10111100b	# 188d	# BCh
# 10011101b	# 157d	# 9Dh		# 10111101b	# 189d	# BDh
# 10011110b	# 158d	# 9Eh		# 10111110b	# 190d	# BEh
# 10011111b	# 159d	# 9Fh		# 10111111b	# 191d	# BFh

Binary	Decimal	Hex.		Binary	Decimal	Hex.
# 11000000b	# 192d	# C0h		# 11100000b	# 224d	# E0h
# 11000001b	# 193d	# C1h		# 11100001b	# 225d	# E1h
# 11000010b	# 194d	# C2h		# 11100010b	# 226d	# E2h
# 11000011b	# 195d	# C3h		# 11100011b	# 227d	# E3h
# 11000100b	# 196d	# C4h		# 11100100b	# 228d	# E4h
# 11000101b	# 197d	# C5h		# 11100101b	# 229d	# E5h
# 11000110b	# 196d	# C6h		# 11100110b	# 230d	# E6h
# 11000111b	# 199d	# C7h		# 11100111b	# 231d	# E7h
# 11001000b	# 200d	# C8h		# 11101000b	# 232d	# E8h
# 11001001b	# 201d	# C9h		# 11101001b	# 233d	# E9h
# 11001010b	# 202d	# CAh		# 11101010b	# 234d	# EAh
# 11001011b	# 203d	# CBh		# 11101011b	# 235d	# EBh
# 11001100b	# 204d	# CCh		# 11101100b	# 236d	# ECh
# 11001101b	# 205d	# CDh		# 11101101b	# 237d	# EDh
# 11001110b	# 206d	# CEh		# 11101110b	# 238d	# EEh
# 11001111b	# 207d	# CFh		# 11101111b	# 239d	# EFh
# 11010000b	# 208d	# D0h		# 11110000b	# 240d	# F0h
# 11010001b	# 209d	# D1h		# 11110001b	# 241d	# F1h
# 11010010b	# 210d	# D2h		# 11110010b	# 242d	# F2h
# 11010011b	# 211d	# D3h		# 11110011b	# 243d	# F3h
# 11010100b	# 212d	# D4h		# 11110100b	# 244d	# F4h
# 11010101b	# 213d	# D5h		# 11110101b	# 245d	# F5h
# 11010110b	# 214d	# D6h		# 11110110b	# 246d	# F6h
# 11010111b	# 215d	# D7h		# 11110111b	# 247d	# F7h
# 11011000b	# 216d	# D8h		# 11111000b	# 248d	# F8h
# 11011001b	# 217d	# D9h		# 11111001b	# 249d	# F9h
# 11011010b	# 218d	# DAh		# 11111010b	# 250d	# FAh
# 11011011b	# 219d	# DBh		# 11111011b	# 251d	# FBh
# 11011100b	# 220d	# DCh		# 11111100b	# 252d	# FCh
# 11011101b	# 221d	# DDh		# 11111101b	# 253d	# FDh
# 11011110b	# 222d	# DEh		# 11111110b	# 254d	# FEh
# 11011111b	# 223d	# DFh		# 11111111b	# 255d	# FFh

B: Graphics Operations and Commands

Setting/Checking Graphics Parameters

Operation (Interactive)	Command (Programmable)	Description
PRG `DSPL` `SIZE` PRG `OBJ` `SIZE`	SIZE	Returns the height and width of the grob, in pixel units (page 103).
→PLOT `RESET`	« 'PPAR' PURGE PICT PURGE PICT DROP »	Resets plot parameters to defaults (page 105).
→PLOT `INDEP`	INDEP	Specifies independent variable (page 106).
→PLOT →`INDEP`	« PPAR 3 GET »	Recalls independent variable (page 106).
→PLOT `DEPN`	DEPND	Specifies dependent variable (page 106).
→PLOT →`DEPN`	« PPAR 7 GET »	Recalls the dependent variable (page 106).
→PLOT `RES`	RES	Specifies the plot resolution (page 106).
→PLOT →`RES`	« PPAR 4 GET »	Recalls plot resolution (page 106).
←MODES `CNCT`	« -31 CF »	Enables curve filling (page 106).

Operation (Interactive)	Command (Programmable)	Description
← MODES **CNCT**	« -31 SF »	Disables the curve filling (page 106).
→ PLOT **AXES**	AXES	Specifies the intersection of axes (page 107).
→ PLOT → **AXES**	« PPAR 4 GET »	Recalls the intersection of axes (page 107).
→ PLOT **CENT**	CENTR	Specifies the center of PICT (page 107).
→ PLOT → **CENT**	« PPAR OBJ→ 6 DROPN + 2 / »	Recalls center of PICT (page 107).
→ PLOT **SCALE**	SCALE	Sets the x and y plotting scales (page 107).
→ PLOT → **SCALE**	« PPAR OBJ→ 6 DROPN SWAP - 10 * C→R PICT SIZE 1 - B→R ROT SWAP / ROT ROT B→R 1 - / SWAP »	Recalls x and y plotting scales (page 107).
→ PLOT **XRNG**	XRNG	Sets the x-axis range (page 108).
→ PLOT → **XRNG**	« PPAR 1 GET RE PPAR 2 GET RE »	Recalls the x-axis range (page 108).
→ PLOT **YRNG**	YRNG	Sets the y-axis range (page 108).

Operation (Interactive)	Command (Programmable)	Description
→PLOT →YRNG	« PPAR 1 GET IM PPAR 2 GET IM »	Recalls y-axis range (page 108).
	PMIN	Sets PMIN (page 108).
	« PPAR 1 GET »	Recalls PMIN (page 108).
	PMAX	Sets PMAX (page 108).
	« PPAR 2 GET »	Recalls PMAX (page 108).
→PLOT PDIM	PDIM	Changes PICT size or user units (page 109).
→PLOT *W	*W	Changes x-axis range (page 109).
→PLOT *H	*H	Changes y-axis range (page 109).

Creation/Manipulation of Grobs

(Graph) STO	« PICT RCL »	Puts PICT onto Stack (pages 89, 112).
(EW) STO	« 0 →GROB »	Turns equation into a grob (pages 89, 112).
PRG DSPL LCD→	LCD→	Turns Stack display into a grob ("snapshot") (pages 89, 112).

Operation (Interactive)	Command (Programmable)	Description
[PRG] **DSPL** **→GRO**	→GROB	Turns any object into a grob (pages 89, 112).
[PRG] **DSPL** **BLAN**	BLANK	Creates a blank grob (pages 89, 112).
	« GROB *x y* 0 »	
[PRG] **DSPL** **GOR**	GOR	Superimposes one grob upon another, OR'ing pixels (page 113).
[PRG] **DSPL** **GXOR**	GXOR	Superimposes one grob upon another, XOR'ing pixels (page 113).
[PRG] **DSPL** **REPL** [PRG] **OBJ** **REPL** (Graphics) **REPL**	REPL	Superimposes one grob upon another, replacing target grob pixels (page 113).
[PRG] **DSPL** **SUB** [PRG] **OBJ** **SUB** (Graphics) **SUB**	SUB	Creates subgrob from parent grob (page 113).
(Graphics) **DEL** (Graphics)[DEL]		Erases ("blanks out") part of grob (page 114).
[→][PLOT]**ERASE** (Graphics)[CLR]	ERASE	Erases (blanks out) all of PICT (page 105).
(Stack) [+]	+	Adds (GOR's) two grobs of same size (page 115).
(Stack) [+/−]	NEG	Inverts a grob, toggling each pixel (page 115).

Accessing, Viewing/Displaying Grobs

Operation (Interactive)	Command (Programmable)	Description
(Stack) ◀ (Stack/CL) GRAPH	GRAPH	Enters graphics environment (page 99).
⇦PLOT **AUTO**	AUTO	(Draws all or some of PICT (pages 89, 105).
⇦PLOT **DRAW**	DRAW	(Draws all or some of PICT (pages 89, 105).
(Graphics) ⇦◀ (EW) ⇦◀	« { } PVIEW «	Enters scrolling mode (page 100).
(Scrolling) ◀,▲,▼,▶		Scrolls through grob. (pages 100, 118-119).
(Scrolling) ⇨◀,⇨▲,⇨▼,⇨▶		Jumps to edge of display or grob (pages 100, 118-119).
(Scrolling) ⇦◀		Exits scrolling mode to EW or graphics (pages 100, 118-119).
(Scrolling) ATTN		Exits scrolling mode to EW or Stack (page 100).
PRG **DSPL** **TEXT** (Graphics) ATTN	TEXT	Exits graphics environment (page 99).
PRG **DSPL** **PVIEW**	PVIEW	Views selected portions of PICT (page 100).
PRG **DSPL** **→LCD**	→LCD	Displays grob in Stack display (page 100).

Editing/Drawing on Grobs

Operation (Interactive)	Command (Programmable)	Description
⊷(PLOT) **AUTO**	AUTO	Plots a curve in PICT. Graphics environment is active. AUTO erases PICT, rescales y-axis, plots axes and the curve (page 105).
⊷(PLOT) **DRAW**	DRAW	Plots a curve in PICT. DRAW does not rescale y-axis. When used in a program, DRAW does not erase PICT or draw axes (page 105).
⊷(PLOT) **DRAX**	DRAX	Draws the x- and y- axes (page 105).
⊷(PLOT) **LABEL**	LABEL	Labels x- and y- axes (or PICT boundaries), using current number format (page 105).
(PRG) **DSPL** **PX→C**	PX→C	Converts pixel coordinates into user units (page 110).
(PRG) **DSPL** **C→PX**	C→PX	Converts user units into pixel coordinates (page 110).
(PRG) **DSPL** **BOX** (Graphics) **BOX**	BOX	Draws a box in PICT (page 110).

Operation (Interactive)	Command (Programmable)	Description
PRG **DSPL** **LINE** (Graphics) **LINE**	LINE	Draws a line in PICT (page 110).
PRG **DSPL** **TLINE** (Graphics) **TLINE**	TLINE	Draws a line in PICT, toggling pixels (page 110).
PRG **DSPL** **ARC** (Graphics) **CIRCL**	ARC	Draws a circle or arc in PICT. **CIRCL** isn't programmable; use a 360° arc (pages 110-111).
PRG **DSPL** **PIXON** (Graphics) **DOT+**	PIXON	Turns a pixel on (page 111).
PRG **DSPL** **PIXOF** (Graphics) **DOT−**	PIXOFF	Turns a pixel off (page 111).
PRG **DSPL** **PIX?**	PIX?	Tests pixel status: 1 = on 0 = off (page 111).

Printing Graphics

Operation (Interactive)	Command (Programmable)	Description
⟵PRINT **PR1**	PR1	Prints grob in Level 1, in graphics mode (page 239).
⟵PRINT **PRVAR**	PRVAR	Prints grob(s) named in Level 1, in graphics mode (page 239).
⟵PRINT **PRST**	PRST	Prints the contents of Stack—grobs in compact mode: Graphics *n*×*m*
⟵PRINT **PRSTC**	PRSTC « ... →STR PR1 ... » « ... 1 →LIST PR1 ... »	Prints a grob in text mode. Note that a list uses less memory than a string.
⟵PRINT **PRLCD** ON-PRINT	PRLCD	Prints display. **Note: Do not use** ON-PRINT with EPSPRINT.LIB or PCLPRINT.LIB (pages 255, 257).

Miscellaneous Graphics Commands

Operation (Interactive)	Command (Programmable)	Description
[PRG] **DSPL** **PICT**	PICT	Specifies the current graphics object. Use « ...PICT RCL... » to put contents onto the Stack.
[PRG] **DSPL** **CLLCD**	CLLCD	Clears (blanks out) the display (page 114).
[PRG] **DSPL** **DISP**	DISP	Displays a line of text (page 114).
[PRG] **DSPL** **FREEZ**	FREEZE	Freezes all or part of the display until next keystroke (page 114).
[←][PLOT] **PTYPE**		Offers user a selection of individual plot types —which are programmable.
(Graphics) [ENTER]		Returns cursor coordinates to Stack.
(Graphics) [+] (Graphics) **COORD**		Displays cursor coordinates in user units. [+], [−] or any menu key will restore menu (page 143).

Operation (Interactive)	Command (Programmable)	Description
(Graphics) ⊟ (Graphics) **KEYS**		Hides/restores Graphics menu. ⊟ or any menu key restores the menu.
(Graphics) ⊠ (Graphics) **MARK**		Marks current cursor location for BOX, LINE, etc.
(Graphics) +/− (Graphics) **+/−**		Toggles cursor style—overwrite vs. invert.
(Graphics) **FCN**		Menu of graphic Solver functions (page 71).
← STAT **BARPL** ← STAT **HISTP** ← STAT **SCATR**	BARPLOT HISTPLOT SCATRPLOT	Generates statistical plots. Refer to the HP Owner's Manual Chapter 21, "Statistics," for more information.

C: User-Named Objects

Alphabetically (objects named by *other objects* are also listed here, among the <u>References</u>)

<u>Name</u>	<u>PATH</u>	<u>References</u>	<u>Page</u>
ADDB	{ HOME TOOLS }		128
AMRT	{ HOME G.CH3 }	PV, FV, N, I, PMT TVoM	80
ARROW	{ HOME TOOLS PICS }		117
BEGEND	{ HOME G.CH3 }	VIEWP	58
BIG	{ HOME TOOLS PICS }		117
BIGSINE	{ HOME TOOLS PICS }		118
BKING	{ HOME TOOLS PICS }		207
BPIECE	{ HOME TOOLS PICS }		207
BULLDOZER	{ HOME TOOLS }	DOZDATA	198
CALEND	{ HOME TOOLS }	MYR	232
CHKRS	{ HOME TOOLS }	Flags, SETUP, REDRAW, GLABEL, MYMOVE, THMOVE, LAYOUT	208
CONTOUR	{ HOME TOOLS }	ARRAY	191
CTR	{ HOME TOOLS }		133
C→L	{ HOME TOOLS }		228
DIODE	{ HOME G.CH3 }	I, V, Vb, Io	67

C: User-Named Objects

By Directory *(Last→First)*

Directory PATH	Name	Directory PATH	Name
{ HOME }	OFF1	**{ HOME TOOLS }**	BULLDOZER
	TOOLS	(cont.)	CONTOUR
	G.CH3		IDID0
	G.CH2		FOURIER
			PLANE
{ HOME TOOLS }	HPRVAR		MULTIPLOT
	HPR1		POINT
	EPRVAR		MAKEFACE
	EPR1		VM
	PRGROB2		Pr8
	⋆ PRGROB1		MkAxis
	FF		Now?
	TRANSLATE		READV
	DISSECT		PSTRIP
	MYR		STRIP
	CALEND		PVU
	MKBOARD		MV
	C→L		SCN
	WHOZAT		PSCN
	MOVEIT		MVall
	VALID		MV10
	HILITE		MV1
	SELECT		NUDGE
	THMOVE		SETUP
	MYMOVE		PSCAN
	REDRAW		SCAN
	STARTUP		
	CHKRS		

Directory PATH	Name	Directory PATH	Name
{ HOME TOOLS } (cont.)	CTR	**{ HOME G.CH3 }**	AMRT
	ADDB		DIODE
	GL→		Step.EQ
	GL↓		MOTION.EQ
	GLABEL		M4
	GRAFX		M3
	RCLPIC		M2
	STOPIC		M1
	GAND		Load.EQ
	TPIX		Wagon
	PVUE		BEGEND
	≠SIZE		MQA
	GSIZE		VIEWP
	SEE		TVoM.EQ
	PICS		REACTOR.EQ
			READP
{ HOME TOOLS PICS }	BKING		POLY
	RKING		TVoM
	BPIECE		R
	RPIECE		IdealGas
	DOZDATA		Fruit
	METER		
	BIGSINE	**{ HOME G.CH2 }**	RLCPER
	ARROW		RLCEXP
	DISPLAY		RLC
	TINY		FOYAY
	NORMAL		
	BIG		
	EMPTY		
	SINE		

Subject Index

(Entries do not include user-named objects—see Appendix C)

Reader Comments

We here at Grapevine like to hear feedback about our books. It helps us produce books tailored to your needs. If you have any specific comments or advice for our authors after reading this book, we'd appreciate hearing from you!

Which of our books do you have?

Comments, Advice and Suggestions:

May we use your comments as testimonials?

Your Name: _____ Profession: _____

City, State: _____

How long have you had your calculator?

Please send Grapevine Catalogues to these persons:

Name _____

Address _____

City _____ State _____ Zip _____

Name _____

Address _____

City _____ State _____ Zip _____

To Order **Grapevine Publications** books:

☎ **Call** to charge the books to **VISA/MasterCard**, *or*

✍ **Send** this Order Form to: **Grapevine Publications, P.O. Box 2449 Corvallis, OR 97339**

Qty.	Item #	Book Title	Unit Cost	Total

Shipping Information:

❏ For orders <u>less</u> than $7 .... **ADD $ 1.00**
   or
❏ **Surface Post** shipping/handling .... **ADD $ 2.50**
   (allow 2-3 weeks for delivery).......................... *or*
❏ **Priority Post** ❏ **UPS** shipping/handling ....**ADD $ 4.00**
   (allow 7-10 days for delivery) .... *or*
❏ **International Air Mail:**
   Add $5 <u>per book</u> to Canada and Mexico. Add $10 <u>per book</u> to all
   other countries (allow 2-3 weeks for delivery).

Subtotal	
Shipping See shipping Info.	
TOTAL	

Payment Information

❏ **Check** enclosed (Please **make your check** payable to **Grapevine Publications, Inc.**)
   (International Check or Money Order must be in U.S. funds and drawn on a U.S. bank)

❏ **VISA** or **MasterCard #** _____ Exp. date _____

Your Signature _____

Name _____ **Phone (** ____ **)** _____

Shipping Address _____

(Note: UPS will not deliver to a P.O. Box! Please give a street address for UPS delivery)

City _____ **State** _____ **Zip** _____ **Country** _____

48 Graphics

Item #	Book Title	Price
	Personal Computer Books	
29	A Little **DOS** Will Do You	$ 9
28	**Lotus** Be Brief	9
32	Concise and **WordPerfect**	9
30	An Easy Course in Using **DOS**	18
38	An Easy Course in Using **Lotus 1-2-3**	18
37	An Easy Course in Using **WordPerfect**	18
40	An Easy Course in Using **dBASE IV**	18
35	The Answers You Need on the **HP 95LX Palmtop PC**	9
34	**Lotus** in Minutes on the **HP 95LX Palmtop PC**	9
	Hewlett-Packard Calculator Books	
19	An Easy Course in Using the **HP 19Bɪɪ**	$ 22
22	The **HP-19B Pocket Guide:** Just In Case	6
20	An Easy Course in Using the **HP-17B**	22
23	The **HP-17B Pocket Guide:** Just In Case	6
05	An Easy Course in Using the **HP-12C**	22
12	The **HP-12C Pocket Guide:** Just In Case	6
31	An Easy Course in Using the **HP 48**	22
33	**HP 48** Graphics	20
18	An Easy Course in Using the **HP-28S**	22
25	**HP-28S** Software Power Tools: **Electrical Circuits**	18
27	**HP-28S** Software Power Tools: **Utilities**	20
26	An Easy Course in Using the **HP-42S**	22
	Curriculum Books	
14	Problem-Solving Situations: A Teacher's Resource Book	$ 15
	Consumer Books	
36	House-Training Your VCR: A Help Manual for Humans	$ 8

(Prices are subject to change without notice)

Grapevine Publications, Inc.

626 N.W. 4th Street   P.O. Box 2449

Corvallis OR, 97339-2449

For orders and order information:

Phone: **1-800-338-4331** (503-754-0583) Fax: **503-754-6508**

About the Author

Ray Depew is a very normal guy who happens to own an HP 48 and likes to write. <u>HP 48 Graphics</u> is his first published work. His other projects in various stages of completion include a compilation of children's stories, additional software for the HP 48, and some musical compositions that may never see the light of day. To make some money on the side, Ray works as an IC engineer for Hewlett-Packard. He lives in Loveland, Colorado, with his wife, five children, and a Dalmatian named "Lazer Jet." When not working, writing, or fixing up the house, he likes to spend time in the Rockies, read, make music, play with his family (and the dog), and eat oatmeal-chocolate chip cookies.

If you have comments or suggestions about this book, he would appreciate hearing them. You can write to him in care of the publisher:

Grapevine Publications, Inc.
P.O. Box 2449
Corvallis, Oregon   97339-2449   U.S.A.